# The If Machine

**Also available from Continuum**

*100 Ideas for Developing Thinking in the Primary School*, Fred Sedgwick

*But Why?*, Sara Stanley & Steve Bowkett

*Teaching Thinking 3rd edition*, Robert Fisher

# The If Machine
## Philosophical Enquiry in the Classroom

### Peter Worley

**Illustrations by Tamar Levi**

continuum

A companion website to accompany this book is available online at:
http://education.worley.continuumbooks.com

Please visit the link and register with us to receive your password and access these downloadable resources.

If you experience any problems accessing the resources, please contact Continuum at: info@continuumbooks.com

**Continuum International Publishing Group**

| | |
|---|---|
| The Tower Building | 80 Maiden Lane |
| 11 York Road | Suite 704 |
| London | New York |
| SE1 7NX | NY 10038 |

www.continuumbooks.com

**British Library Cataloguing-in-Publication Data**
A catalogue record for this book is available from the British Library.

ISBN: 978-1-4411-5583-2 (paperback)

**Library of Congress Cataloging-in-Publication Data**
Worley, Peter.
 The if machine : philosophical enquiry in the classroom / Peter Worley ; illustrations by Tamar Levi.
   p. cm.
 ISBN 978-1-4411-5583-2 (pbk.) -- ISBN 978-1-4411-1240-8 (ebook (pdf)) -- ISBN 978-1-4411-9228-8 (ebook (epub)) 1. Critical thinking--Study and teaching (Elementary) 2. Reflective learning. 3. Children and philosophy. I. Title.
 LB1590.3.W67 2011
 370.15'2--dc22

                          2010031208

Typeset by Fakenham Photosetting Ltd
Printed and bound in Great Britain

For my parents Ian, Lorraine, and my parents-in-law, Chris and Jocelyn whose support, at different times, has been invaluable.

'Education to independence demands that young people should be accustomed early to consult their own sense of propriety and their own reason.'

G.W.F Hegel (1770–1831)

# Contents

# Acknowledgements

I would like to thank the following people for their help and assistance in completing this book

My editor at Continuum, Melanie Wilson, whose advice has been invaluable in this, my first attempt at writing a book. Thank you to Tamar Levi for her close reading of the text and her accompanying advice on everything from grammar and format to style. I would also like to thank Tamar for the lovely illustrations that pepper the pages. Thanks go to Julie Odege, Amanda Crook and Annette Gordon at John Ball Primary School for each casting their teacher's eyes over the manuscript and to Oliver Leech for his eyes: one philosopher's eye and one teacher's eye. A big 'thank you' to the schools, head teachers, teachers and children with whom I work for giving me the opportunity to test and develop all these sessions and particularly to the children for finding the holes I failed to see. Thank you to all the consultants at The Philosophy Shop and especially to Robert Torrington and Ruth Oswald for their ideas in *Republic Island* and to Andrew Day and Miriam Cohen for general feedback on the sessions themselves. I would like to thank head teacher Kathy Palmer for encouraging and allowing me to try out the philosophy idea in the school right at the beginning and for taking me in as a staff member of Eliot Bank School. Finally, I would like to thank my wife Emma for all her incredible work for The Philosophy Shop, for the book and for me. In all respects she is quite simply my *sine qua non*.

# Preface

This is a book with a split personality. Is it a method or is it a classroom resource? In the end I have had to concede that it is a mixture of the two. There has to be some explanation before one can commence with the sessions but, given the time teachers have for ploughing through pages of theory and text, I have had to compromise on the extent to which this is a method while trying to retain what Aristotle would call the essential features. For this reason I have tried to sneak the method upon the reader with the use of boxes to introduce techniques and hints during the preparation for each session. The genesis of the book itself has been highly collaborative with the children and with their keen analytic faculties they have often, during the process of taking part in a session, helped me to sharpen some of the questions. For example, in the story 'The Prince and the Pig' the Prince's wish was, originally, 'I wish I was a pig, then I would be happy'. One of the children (aged 7) pointed out that: 'Just being a pig doesn't mean that he would be happy'. In other words, and in more pompous language, it does not necessarily follow that a pig will be happy by virtue of being a pig. As a result of this perceptive remark I changed the wish to 'I wish I was a happy pig'. There are many other such examples and I am sure there are some that have not yet been detected by my unofficial proofreaders. But this does provide a wonderful example of the level of thinking of which primary school children are capable.

Doing philosophy and the accompanying thinking that this entails is like entering a maze, and at various times in this book I have used this metaphor to illustrate what the role of the facilitator involves. In the Ancient Greek myth *Theseus and the Minotaur*, Ariadne helps Theseus defeat the Minotaur and escape from the maze by leaving him a thread. There are two important features of this metaphor that are relevant to the facilitator's role. First, Ariadne enables him to keep track of where he has come from even though the maze is complex, and second she is not present while he navigates the maze. Though she provides the tools he has to do the rest himself. With regard to facilitation, these two themes of *navigation* and *absence* are the *idée fixes* of this book and I would urge you to keep them in mind at all times while you read the book. Keep asking yourself these questions: 'Am I too involved in the discussion?'. 'Do the children know where they are in the discussion?'. 'How can I facilitate greater understanding without telling them?' General warning signs are: if they know what you think or if you are telling them what they think then you need to rethink. On that note I shall leave you with this: heed this advice from one of the (lamentably) only two women mentioned in this book.

# Table of Sessions

## Star Ratings

\* Easy
\*\* Moderate
\*\*\* More difficult

The star ratings are here to give you a guide as to the difficulty level of the session. This is not necessarily age related. For example, The Ceebie Stories can all be used with children aged 7 and upwards, but some of the sessions will be more challenging than others. The key to dealing with challenging sessions is clarity of presentation. Make sure that you are familiar with the sessions and that you understand them yourself. Do not be afraid to try a more difficult session with your class: you will often find that your class surprise you.

| Session title | Themes | Page | Age | Star rating |
|---|---|---|---|---|
| The Chair | Things and what they are to us<br>Perception<br>Points of view<br>Names and referring terms | 49 | 7< | \*\* |
| The Meaning of Ant Life | Purpose and design<br>Existentialism<br>God and religion<br>Value | 57 | 9< | \*\* |
| Can You Step in the Same River Twice? | Change<br>Arguments<br>Identity<br>Necessary and sufficient conditions<br>Rivers and water cycles | 61 | 8< | \* |

| Session title | Themes | Page | Age | Star rating |
|---|---|---|---|---|
| The Shadow of the Pyramid | Arguments<br>Wisdom<br>Problem-solving<br>Sophistry | 117 | 9< | ** |
| Billy Bash | Self-control<br>Emotions<br>Belief<br>Happiness | 128 | 6< | * |
| Thinking About Nothing | Existence<br>Language<br>Reference<br>Meaning<br>Numbers<br>Maths<br>Ancient Greece | 135 | 8< | ** |
| Yous on Another Planet | Personal identity<br>Identity<br>Humanity | 139 | 10< | *** |
| The Ceebie Stories: Friends | Friendship<br>Relationships<br>Empathy | 144 | 7< | * |
| The Ceebie Stories: The Tony Test | Artificial intelligence<br>Computing<br>Thinking<br>Language | 149 | 7< | ** |
| The Ceebie Stories: The Robbery | Responsibility<br>Knowledge<br>History<br>Choice | 155 | 7< | *** |
| The Ceebie Stories: The Android | Being human<br>Analogy<br>Personal identity | 162 | 7< | * |
| The Ceebie Stories: The Lie | Dilemmas<br>Decision-making<br>Values<br>Friendship<br>Lying | 166 | 7< | *** |

# Section 1:
## How to Do Philosophical Enquiry in the Classroom

# Introduction

## Who is this book for?

This book has been written as a resource for anyone who wants to do philosophy with children in schools, youth groups or other settings. The material has been gathered from nearly 10 years of experience doing **philosophy** (you will find words in bold briefly explained in the glossary on page 191) with children from ages 5–13, and is suitable for use with children of this age and range of abilities. If you have not studied philosophy then please note that this book and online material have been written to provide an introduction to the relevant philosophical material. This aims to give you a basic philosophical awareness so that you can feel more confident and get more out of the philosophy sessions in your class. This book also aims to serve as a general introduction to philosophy as a subject, and hopes to spark your interest to learn and read more about it.

One great thing about philosophy is that children do not need to be familiar with it to be able to do it. To be able to facilitate philosophic discussions, however, it helps to have a basic awareness of the philosophical topics and debates that surround the sessions provided in this book. This will help you to encourage – or to identify – philosophical insights from the children. These, in turn, will help you to navigate the philosophical direction of the sessions. It is important to be aware that philosophy is much more than simply talking together and sharing ideas: it is a certain *kind* of thinking about certain *kinds* of topics (see 'philosophy' in the glossary). The kind of thinking that philosophy practises, however, can be applied to almost any subject. At the beginning of each session I have included a quick summary introduction of the philosophy that lies behind it, and at the end a guide to further reading available on the companion website that accompanies this book.

Do remember that the information about philosophy you find in this book and the companion website is *not* information to be taught to children in the philosophy sessions; it is there to help you develop a philosophical awareness to help with the facilitation of the sessions. In other words, it assists you to be able to spot the philosophy in the sessions and guide the discussion appropriately. From this point on, while you are reading this book and doing philosophy with children, you are not a teacher, you are a 'curious facilitator'. By this I mean that you are as interested in the ideas being discussed as the children and will do all you can to help the children explore ideas, but you will not be teaching them as you would in your normal role as 'teacher' and you will not be expressing your own ideas.

If you do philosophy regularly with your class and become familiar with the methods and teaching strategies (page 29) in this book you may find it can impact and inform your normal class teaching. This happens by developing transferable skills in the children such as speaking and listening, reasoning, questioning, autonomous learning, as well as critical and creative thinking. The teaching strategies should also help you to develop your teaching by giving you greater confidence with questioning and discourse skills, engendering a more collaborative relationship with your class and an atmosphere of active learning and **enquiry**. These areas of development have been shown to play a crucial role in creating independent learners in students.

# The structure of this book

This book has two sections and a companion website. The first section, 'How to do **Philosophical Enquiry** in the Classroom', begins with an introduction to the subject of philosophy with children, and outlines my philosophical enquiry method (PhiE). There is then a full and comprehensive list of the teaching strategies that are covered in this book. These strategies can be used in any educational setting to help deepen thinking by developing questioning skills that will elicit more from the children, and engage the children critically with the material and with each other.

The second section, 'The PhiE Sessions', contains 25 sessions on different philosophical topics. The sessions are designed to last 1 hour, and can be extended over more than one session depending on how much discussion is generated by the questions and enquiries. Some sessions such as *The Chair*, *Republic Island*, *Billy Bash* and *Shadow of the Pyramid* are designed to span more than one session. Where this is the case, it is clearly marked at the beginning of the session. Each session includes a series of boxes that draw your attention to various features. These features include Teaching Strategy, Philosophy, Hints and Tips, Extension Activities and Related Sessions. These can be easily identified by the icons shown below.

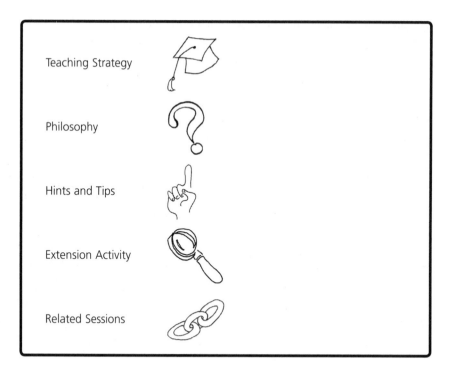

| Teaching Strategy | |
| Philosophy | |
| Hints and Tips | |
| Extension Activity | |
| Related Sessions | |

The companion website that accompanies this book includes a comprehensive explanation of key terms used in the book, a guideline list of criteria for philosophical aptitude that children can develop through doing the philosophy sessions, and a sample PhiE session with descriptions of facilitation and Speaker Management methods to give you a context for their use. Illustrations that accompany the sessions can be downloaded as a visual supplement for the stimuli, and you will find some selected arguments, indicated in the book, also available for download. Additionally, the website provides an introduction to the philosophy that inspired the sessions. These 'philosophy nuggets' include the following.

- Philosopher and topic: the philosopher and the topic behind the session.
- Biography: a brief outline of the history of the philosopher.
- Big idea: a bite-size version of the relevant idea associated with the philosopher.
- Main publication(s): a reference to the most well-known publication(s) or the one most relevant to the topic. Interested readers are advised to seek these as further reading.
- Useful quote: a short quote from a primary source that captures the philosopher's view on the relevant topic.

- About: a short discussion about the philosopher and the topic.
- Food for thought: this section is designed to get the reader thinking and engaging with the philosophical questions and issues that arise from the philosopher's idea. Dine on them with your friends to properly engage with these ideas.

# How to use this book

To use this book, begin by reading Section 1 thoroughly before trying to run a session. In Section 2 (page 47) the sessions can generally be used in whatever order you like. *The Ceebie Stories* are different from the other sessions in that they have a continuous narrative that connects them. For this reason it is important that they be done successively. Do not try to run *The Ceebie Stories* in isolation from each other as there is too much background information that is not included in each individual session. There is a table for quick reference on page xiii, which includes a list of themes present in the sessions, age suitability and a star rating for difficulty that will also appear at the top of each session. On the next page you will see an example session detailing the different sections of a session.

# Can You Step in the Same River Twice?

Each session has a title, and begins with the star rating, guidance as to the age-group suitability of the session and a list of broad themes that the session addresses.

Suitable for age 8 and upwards.
Star rating: *

## Themes

Change
Arguments
Identity

This is followed by an introduction to the philosophical themes, issues and topics that lie behind or that may arise from the session.

## Philosophy

This is one of the most famous philosophical questions and it is thought to have been first asked by Heraclitus of Ephesus (fl. c. 500 BCE) ...

Next is the **Stimulus**, followed by the **Task Question**(s) (TQs) you should ask along with notes and guidance for the facilitator on how to run the session plus what they might expect from the children.

## Stimulus

*Timmy and Tina have gone to a river with their parents for a picnic and they are paddling in the river close to the riverbank swishing their fishing nets around trying to catch tadpoles ...*

> TQ: Can you say why Tina thinks it is a different river?

Give them **Talk Time** with their partners and find out what they think. If they are not having the Heraclitian insight, 'that it is not the same river because the water is constantly flowing', then you could present an argument between the two characters to bring this out ...

There will be a box or boxes containing a Teaching Strategy, Hints and Tips, Philosophy, or an Extension Activity. The teaching strategies are described more generally in the Teaching Strategies section but given a specific context in the boxes in the sessions, thereby giving clear examples of their use.

### Teaching Strategy: What's needed and what's enough? (page 29)

One line of enquiry following this is to explore with the children what makes a river. Do a *what's needed and what's enough?* strategy with them on 'what is a river?' Write the word 'river' on the board, and then set them the task of listing all the features a river would need to be a river ...

The introduction to the philosophy given at the beginning of the session is supplemented on the companion website. At the end of each session you will be directed to the main online philosophy for the session, and also a series of related online philosophy topics.

## Online

Main philosophy:
Heraclitus and Change

Related philosophy:
Berkeley and Idealism
Hobbes and Materialism
Leibniz and Identity

> Finally, a Related Sessions box lists sessions with common philosophical themes for those interested in following Ariadne's threads through the book (see Teaching Strategies, page 29).

 **Related Sessions**

The Chair (page 49)
The Ship of Theseus (page 86)

The PhiE sessions will not necessarily unfold in the way described in the book, but I have attempted to share my experience with ideas and problems that commonly occur in the sessions. Also, I have included some directions that the sessions have taken in order to share a teaching strategy.

# The If Machine

## The art of 'iffing'

My method of *iffing* (that is, the reframing of questions or sentences into the 'if ... then ...' form) is the central idea of this book and is also implicitly present in many of the teaching strategies described. Compare these two versions of the same question:

1 It is okay to eat meat so why don't we eat our pets?
2 *If* it is okay to eat meat *then* why don't we eat our pets?

The second formulation is in the conditional form (if ... then ...) and it enables the discussion to side-step the contentious facts in order to follow the material that is of philosophical or conceptual interest. It does not matter what individuals in the group each think about whether it is okay to eat meat in B because it simply asks us to imagine that it is okay to eat meat so that we can consider what might follow from this. This method does not commit anyone to the view that it is okay to eat meat, simply to entertain it for the purposes of the discussion.

The method of *iffing* is a kind of **hypothetical thinking**, which asks us to imagine a situation that might not be the case in order to think about what it would mean for us. Hypothetical thinking also highlights that philosophy is as much about imaginative thinking as it is about logical thinking. My method of facilitating philosophy with children could be summarised as the cultivation of the art of iffing.

The activity of hypothetical thinking is an essential part of the activity of philosophy as a whole. Whereas science tests hypotheses factually, philosophy tests hypotheses conceptually. Or, to put it another way, science asks, 'Is it *true* that so-and-so ...?', whereas philosophy asks, 'Does it make *sense* that so-and-so ...?' And crucial to asking this question is the use of the conditional question.

Hypothetical thinking is one important criterion for the identification of what I call *philosophical aptitude*. Online you will find a list (though not necessarily exhaustive) of children's philosophical aptitude with examples taken from real sessions. This list provides basic criteria for identifying children who may already possess philosophical aptitude, but it also highlights the areas that children who do philosophy can hope to develop. Notice that philosophical aptitude is distinct from a straightforwardly gifted and talented child – that is, a bright child may or may not have the skills listed. As a result, philosophy can help to identify gifted and talented children not hitherto identified by the usual methods because it requires a different kind of approach to thinking.

# Why teach philosophy?

Research has shown that regular philosophical enquiry increases problem-solving skills, cognitive ability, critical reasoning, confidence, communication, generating alternative solutions and decision-making (East Renfrewshire Psychological Services, 2006; Dundee University, 2007). The Dundee research also showed an increase of pupil IQ by 6.5 points. In addition to the list of more familiar benefits conferred by philosophy I would like to offer a few of my own reflections on why we should teach philosophy in our schools.

'In philosophy sometimes there are no answers and sometimes there are loads of possible answers but you don't know which one's right.'
Year 6 pupil at John Ball Primary School, Lewisham.

It is often said that philosophy's virtue is that it has no right-and-wrong answers, so one can't be wrong in philosophy. I don't think it's accurate that one can't be wrong in philosophy: one can misunderstand someone else's argument, say something contradictory or construct a **fallacious argument**. Conversely, I think it would be wrong to tell children that there are right answers and to reward the children when it is thought they have provided them, not least because it is so difficult with philosophy to decide what the right answers might be. So what's needed is a forum that allows the children to explore ideas, make mistakes on the way and recognise that mistakes have been made without the facilitator at any point telling them they are 'wrong'. The key to tackling this difficulty lies in self-evaluation and autonomous thinking – two important virtues that emerge from doing philosophy. First of all, it is not for the facilitator to decide what thinking is right or wrong, it is for the children to think for themselves and to come to their own conclusions based on the best reasons they have heard or thought of, and to be aware that their conclusions may change with time. In this way the children learn how to evaluate solutions for themselves rather than having to rely on hearing the 'right answer' from the teacher. Conversely, neither are they complacent that everything they say is 'right' simply by virtue of having expressed their opinion.

**Figure 1:** Right way vs my map

The status of philosophy is such that it is not the case that you cannot be wrong in philosophy but that it is very difficult to be right. The questions in philosophy are often the questions that remain unanswered by other disciplines such as science or religion – not necessarily because they have failed to answer these questions but because the kind of question that is typically philosophical in character is not the kind of question these subjects are equipped to answer. This is why it remains within the jurisdiction of philosophy. However, because philosophy makes use of the application of argument and reasoning, philosophy can be said to recognise *good reasoning* and *bad reasoning* and it is in this sense that you can be 'wrong' in philosophy. It does not have the kinds of answers that can be treated as 'right answers' in the sense that other subjects such as English or maths do; the emphasis in philosophy is the *process* of thinking about something rather than the outcome of that process. So, though philosophising is often inconclusive it would be mistaken to think that it is a thinking process incapable of error: one is able to contradict oneself or to construct a fallacious argument without necessarily having resolved the question or problem.

## Autonomous thinking

A philosophy session is the perfect forum for 'thinking for yourself' and during this session the children should be allowed to both think things through for themselves and to 'get things wrong' without condemnation. This means that the facilitator has to resist temptation to explain what they see as the right answer. Another good reason for resisting this temptation is that what the facilitator sees as 'the right answer' may itself be open to legitimate criticism though the facilitator may not have noticed. This is ever more the case when the subject is philosophy. Even if it is felt by the teacher that it is not appropriate to adopt this attitude at all times, it should be adopted at least during the PhiE or enquiry session each week.

## Self-evaluation

A very important skill is not *how to get the right answer* but *how to identify and evaluate an answer*. Many children will want to know what the answer is at the end of a session, but when dealing with the sorts of questions you will find in this book, if the teacher were to say what they think is the right answer, it would be very unlikely that the children would be unanimous in their agreement with this. In this way the debate should continue. Once the children have the ability to evaluate an answer, then if a teacher were to provide an answer to a question, the children will have been empowered to be able to *assess* the answer given by the teacher. Teachers can be wrong after all, and books do have misprints.

---

Here are some sample questions to be used with the children on the topic of right and wrong answers to be used during inevitable discussions about 'what the answer is'.

- If the teacher were to tell you what they thought was the right answer, would you have to agree with them?
- If a teacher or a book provides you with the right answer, how do you know if it's right?

Imagine the following scenario.

> A teacher asks two children the answer to this question: 'What is 2 + 2?' The first child says '4'. When asked 'Why?' he replies, 'Because it's my lucky number.' The second child says '5' and when asked 'Why?' she explains that she counted on her fingers but it turns out that she made an error in calculation.

Question: Who has given the best answer and why?

---

# Philosophical Enquiries in the Classroom

PhiE provides you with a method for bringing philosophy to children that includes some important features of the activity of philosophy (see the Philosophical Aptitude list online). As with other methods of doing philosophy with children, the emphasis is on them learning to philosophise. This means that the children will be *doing* philosophy, or actively engaging in the processes of thinking that characterises philosophy as an academic subject. In addition to this the children will also learn something of the history of philosophy by engaging critically with the ideas of some philosophers. The facilitation skills, Speaker Management and Teaching Strategies contained in the PhiE method have been developed to actively encourage philosophical thinking, and to distinguish this kind of thinking from that of other discussion-based approaches, for example Circle Time. The PhiE method also makes use of a philosophical device known as **'thought experiments'**.

## What thought experiments are and setting the philosophical arena

There is a commonly held opinion, based on **Deweyan** principles, that philosophy with children must be democratic and that the children must choose the questions to explore around a story or stimulus. Stories are often used to stimulate these questions but it is important to understand that a 'story' is different from a 'thought experiment' and that the approach to question selection will inevitably be different as a result.

The way children may respond to a story can vary hugely; they can be stimulated philosophically, emotionally or any number of ways. However, a thought experiment is designed to stimulate thinking in a particular way: they are used by philosophers and scientists to test the implications of a theory or an idea, and to test the limits and implications of the **concepts** involved. Here is an example of a thought experiment, told simply and without frills, with some accompanying questions.

> *Imagine Tom discovers that he was once someone else called Jeff. Jeff was a bad person who committed all sorts of crimes but an operation was performed on him to remove Jeff's memories and to have them replaced with a new set of fictional memories of an entirely different kind of person: those of Tom. Tom is a good, law-abiding citizen.*
>
> - Who would you consider this person to be: Tom or Jeff?
> - And, should Tom be held morally responsible for any crimes committed by Jeff?

This thought experiment has been designed to test our conceptual intuitions about a specific issue: it leads us to think about how we conceive of the self and to consider what role memory plays in our understanding of ourselves.

Many, though not all, of the stories contained in this volume are inspired by classic thought experiments from philosophy, and for this reason I have opted to be more directive in the setting of Task Questions, eschewing the democratic approach to question selection in order to reach the intended philosophical arena of the thought experiment. Having said this, I do think that the child-centred approach to doing philosophy should also be preserved once the philosophical arena has been established. In other words, one should follow the children and draw out from them new questions and lines of philosophical inquiry to move the discussions forward (see **Emergent Questions** online and in the glossary).

## Setting up the space

Discussions are often best conducted in a circle, oval or horse-shoe shape so that the children can see each other during the discussion; this helps to improve the **dialogue** element to the discussions. I prefer the horse-shoe shape to the circle because it enables the facilitator to access the board if necessary, and I find that the board is an essential visual aid to the children's understanding.

Within this book I have suggested many times that a diagram be drawn to help the children with an idea; the board is necessary for this, so the facilitator will need to be able to access it easily. In terms of learning styles the stories are auditory, so the diagrams provide a visual aspect to their understanding. Where possible, the diagrams and concept maps should be recorded. So if you are using an interactive whiteboard, save your diagrams in a 'philosophy' or 'enquiry' file; this will help with continuing discussions that carry over several weeks. I also often use a ball that the children hold so they can see easily whose turn it is to speak. The ball should be soft and not bouncy – as least distracting a tool as possible. Once the children become more expert at the philosophy discussions, then this could be phased out, but you need to be careful about how this is done. (See *Self-Management* in the Speaker Management section on page 27).

A word about the format: many teachers find the circle or horse-shoe shape inconvenient because it requires a complete restructure of the classroom for the purpose of conducting only the philosophy sessions. One teacher/philosophy consultant colleague of mine has solved this problem and – in his view – improved the overall learning in his classroom by permanently restructuring the classroom to follow the horse-shoe structure, including desks. This, he says, enables all his teaching to make use of the enquiry model. You will notice that the significantly improved quality of the discussions as a result of taking this measure will justify the small amount of trouble it may take to move the classroom around.

## The PhiE model

The facilitator instructions will give you a detailed guideline of how to run each of the sessions. However, the basic PhiE model is as follows.

**Figure 2:** The talk ball

Step 1: First of all you will need to present the **stimulus** by reading out the relevant passage from the session.

Step 2: Carry out **First Thoughts**, **Talk Time** and **Comprehension Time** if necessary. Allow a short period of uninfluenced reflection from the children – perhaps some time to talk to each other about the story with no particular objective, followed by any questions, thoughts or ideas they have about what they've heard. Then spend a short time sharing these thoughts and allow other children to answer any questions asked. This can help with comprehension before the main enquiry begins. This is also where you may find an Emergent Task Question.

Step 3: Set the **Task Question** and display on the board for all to see.

Step 4: Give the children some **Talk Time** (from 2 to 5 minutes) to discuss the Task Question in pairs or small groups. The facilitator should use this opportunity to engage with some of the groups, though there will not be time to engage with all the pairs or groups.

Step 5: Allow children to share their ideas with the whole class or group in an **enquiry**. Here, they can build on and develop their ideas in the context of collaborative group exploration on the issues and topics under consideration. Make use of Talk Time during the enquiry to keep the pace of the session up and to channel their energy in the right way. (See Facilitation, page 19 and Speaker Management, page 22 for how to conduct and manage an enquiry).

Step 6: If there are more Task Questions, then repeat steps 3–5 using another Task Question. Sometimes you will find a suitable Task Question emerges from the discussion itself.

This is a general model and you will notice that, for many reasons, many of the sessions do not strictly follow this model. There are sessions where *first thoughts* is not included because it is essential that the prepared Task Question be used to propel the session into the philosophy immediately; and in some of the sessions there may be no need for comprehension-time, i.e. in *The Chair* (page 49).

# Stimulus

The stimulus for each session is mostly in the form of a story. That said, in some cases you will find a dialogue (see *Get Stuffed: Fun with Metaphysics*, page 186) or activities (see *Republic Island*, page 66). The stories may be read as they are, but you will find that, as written, they are not always appropriate for all the age groups indicated at the beginning of each session. You may simply replace some of the more sophisticated words with simpler ones ('perimeter' could become 'edge' or 'lush' could become 'green') or you could leave out unnecessary words altogether ('featureless' or 'darkly'). I like to use words that the children may not know to encourage their use and also to give them the opportunity to infer the meaning of words from a context. Alternatively, I may quickly explain a word's meaning if I feel it is essential for understanding the story. Apart from the occasional omission of descriptive words it is important to stick to the written version as it may have been specifically designed to accurately pinpoint a particular philosophical issue through the plot structure or the set-up of a scene (see 'What thought experiments are and setting the philosophical arena', page 14).

## Comprehension Time

With a story it is often a good idea to simply spend some time making sense of it all. Allow 'Comprehension Time' after finishing a more involved story, e.g. *The Ceebie Stories: The Lie*, page 166 or *Yous on Another Planet* page 139; sometimes you may even want to read it twice, though this is not usually necessary. The first task you could set the children is that they retell the story as a group. The first person recounts what they can remember or speaks until you stop them, and then you simply ask the others if they can add something that 'has not been said already'. It is important to say this or it could take far too long and lose the children's interest. After a few contributions class members usually have a pretty comprehensive overview of the events in the story. Sometimes the discussion will follow naturally from Comprehension Time, but if not then move on to the prepared Task Question in the session.

## Diagrams

Sometimes diagrams are important for the facilitation of the children's understanding before you begin the enquiry. I have provided examples of the diagrams where necessary. It is important to draw the diagram *as you explain the scenario back to the class* because this is the best way for the children to follow any complex situations (see *The Ceebie Stories: The Lie*, page 166). If you simply project a ready-drawn diagram onto the board it is less likely to mean anything to the children. Hearing the story is largely an auditory learning experience, so the diagrams add a visual element for the visual learners in the class.

**Figure 3:** Visual, Auditory, Kinaesthetic

# Facilitation

Reading the session and presenting the children with the stimulus is just the starting point for a successful session. The success will depend very much on the facilitation skills of the teacher. It is difficult to teach these skills in a book but here are some guidelines to help keep you on the right track. Some facilitation techniques are included below; if you would like further training please see the end pages of this book (pages 196–197) for details.

## Clarification questions

Ask lots of these, such as: 'Can you say more?' 'What do you mean by … ?' and 'Could you explain that again in different words?' Children often take time to express themselves and it is up to you to get them to do this without putting words in their mouth.

## The 'waiter approach'

Resist the temptation to say what you think. A teacher once said to me that the difficult thing for her, when running an enquiry, would be to resist expressing her opinions. As I told her, 'It is not just a problem *for you*: it is *the* problem.' Running a PhiE session is an ego-suppressing exercise. When you are a facilitator you, as a personality, are not present. You will challenge the children in certain specific ways such as with role-play or tension play etc., but the facilitator should never challenge personally. The reasons for this quickly become apparent when you fail to resist the temptation. Once the facilitator has said what they think many of the children will identify this view as 'the right answer' (this is how they are trained to think thus far in schools) and will echo that idea so that the natural diversity that normally inhabits a PhiE session will disappear. If, when the children start the enquiry following Talk Time, you find that the children say: 'You said ...' (or words to that effect), it is a good clue that you have been saying too much about your opinions during Talk Time. I call this the *ego-detector*. Like a good waiter, a good facilitator, is 'present but hidden': the facilitation skills should be present but the ego hidden.

## Time and space to think

Ask questions clearly, one at a time, and give the children plenty of time to formulate their responses. To understand how this works pick up a book of poetry and read some of the poems at random. Notice how, very often, a poem means very little the first time you read it; you need to stop and think, to re-read certain passages. You need to 'soak it up' and give yourself time to let the images form in your mind. The poem can still be processing days after the first reading. Some children think quickly but many need time to let the ideas formulate and then still more time to find an expression for those ideas. One of the most common pieces of feedback I receive from teachers who observe the PhiE sessions is that they realise they need to give children more time to think when they ask them questions. Teachers are often advised to give at least three seconds wait time between a question and a response. I sometimes wait for up to a minute. Give them time to think. Occasionally, a small prompt such as an *anchor* of some kind (see *The Chair*, page 49 or Teaching Strategies, page 29) may be needed to remind the child what it is they are thinking about. Very often a child is too embarrassed to say they have forgotten and will sit there appearing to think about the question when, in fact, they are not.

## Echo

Echo the children's ideas when necessary and keep it as close to their own words as possible. Echoing is different from paraphrasing, as paraphrasing changes the wording. Also, do not tell them 'You are saying ...' when you echo. Ask them a question: 'Are you saying ...?' Be open to having them correct you. Very often, especially with younger children, you will have to echo what they say simply because they don't say it loud enough for the entire group to hear. Echoing is also useful for keeping an idea present within the group or when you want to link ideas or contrast them.

## Remember

Try to remember who said what and when. Knowing which idea came from which person is essential if you want the group to be able to refer to each other and build on each other's ideas at a later stage.

## Mapping

Mentally map the locations of ideas during an enquiry. Once you have remembered who said what, you need to be able to establish how ideas relate so that you can refer the children to each other when necessary, allowing the discussion to develop philosophically. (See also *echoing*.)

## Link

Link the children's comments and ideas: Sometimes children will do an excellent job of linking their ideas together, but other times you will need to make some of the links explicit. Link ideas that are similar but also that challenge one another: 'So, what do you think of Alice's earlier point that …?' (See also *tension play*, page 24.)

## Be prepared

Have ready back-up Task Questions, **Nested Questions** and any activities. Experience will tell you where discussions can go and the avenues they will usually take. The sessions in this book include a list of Nested Questions, but you may well think of more so jot them down.

## Elicit

Ask yourself: 'Is there another way that I can find out more about what the children mean?' When a child says something, what they say is only the end-point of a thinking process so, as a facilitator, you should be keen to elicit more of why they have said what they have said. Do not force this; you must be gentle. So, if you ask some elicitation questions and the child looks unable to offer any more, then leave them. You can always come back to them at a later stage.

## Rules of facilitation

There are some basic rules of facilitating a PhiE session so that the children learn to trust each other and to challenge each other respectfully.

- Always ask questions to answer their direct questions to you. For example, 'Does anyone think they can answer that?' or 'What do you think?' Feign ignorance on an issue in order to develop the discussion. This principle is called **Socratic irony** (after the philosopher **Socrates**).
- Never make them feel inadequate.
- Don't tell them if you think they are wrong. Instead, ask them questions so that they might rethink their position or, better still, facilitate other children to do this.
- As often as possible, let the children challenge each other's ideas rather than doing it yourself. You will often find they do this rather well if you give them the opportunity.
- Cultivate an environment of respect, one where they feel that they can speak without fear and are able to disagree with each other respectfully.
- It can be useful to have a philosophical or conceptual aim of where you want the session to go but resist any temptations to take it there yourself. If the children don't achieve the goal you were aiming for sometimes you have to accept this.

# Speaker Management

One of the main problems a facilitator faces is how to manage the speakers in the PhiE group. There will be those who want to speak a great deal and those who want to remain silent, as well as those who want to speak but will only do so when they feel comfortable in the setting. Your aim will be to try to increase the frequency with which everybody contributes and to have a more even distribution of contributions. Another of your aims will be to see developments in terms of the quality of the contributions. This can be anything from deeper philosophical insights to simply providing supporting reasons, or, a normally quiet child speaking out more comfortably. Here is a list of the PhiE method Speaker Management techniques.

## Invitation

Invite everyone to speak and make it known that you are interested in their own ideas and thoughts. Use Talk Time to discover different ideas and listen out for interesting new ones. Then invite those initial ideas to start off the group enquiry.

## Silent engagement

Not contributing out loud does not necessarily mean that a child is not engaged. This is not to say that you shouldn't encourage them to speak, just that there is no rush. Use Talk Time to find out what they think, then you will know if they are, in fact, engaging with the discussion.

## Free play

This is where there is a free-for-all and whoever wants to speak is invited to put up their hand. This avoids artificiality and is often the best way to get things going. When using free play, try to choose speakers fairly – in other words, choose speakers who have not already spoken.

## Paired primers

It is often useful to begin by inviting pairs or groups to share their ideas before using free play, especially if there are disagreements within the group. This can act as a good stimulus for the rest of the class, as it can reveal controversies (see *Revealing Controversies*, page 39).

## Mini dialogue within an enquiry

The idea behind the paired primer can be developed further by inviting a larger group who have been discussing together in Talk Time to conduct their own enquiry while remaining class members observe. This can be left to run its own course for a minute or two.

## Hands-up rule

Begin with a *hands-up-to-speak* rule. Make sure the children also know they must put down their hands when someone is thinking or speaking. This will need regular reiteration before they make it a habit. Tell them at the outset that sometimes you will ask them to put down their hands (see *random selection* below).

## Random selection

This is where you ask the children to put their hands down and pass a ball to someone making sure that person knows that if they have nothing to say or don't want to speak they can pass the ball back again. This is a good opportunity to give the 'silent members' a chance to speak without having to wait for them to put up their hands (which some will never do, given half a chance).

## Speaker choice

Another strategy is to allow the person holding the ball to choose the next speaker once they have finished. I find this a little problematic, as they often choose their friends which can foster resentment and make the children agitated. But, used sparingly this can be good. I use this strategy most often in the following circumstance.

## Peer support

If someone becomes 'stuck' and unable to finish their thought, ask them if there is someone in the class who they think could help.

## Right to reply

If someone makes a comment about something somebody has said then I use this rule. This gives the person whose idea has been talked about an immediate opportunity to respond, either to defend their position or even to rethink it. The children generally accept this contravention of equal distribution of contributions if they know beforehand that it is in operation. It is also a good way to deepen thinking in discussions. This is one of the techniques that children may be explicitly told about.

## Rounds

Use a *rounds* system where you allow each child one contribution in a round. A round could be defined by 'answers given to one particular question or discussion'. This is best implemented when using the *free play* method.

## Frequency detection

At a certain point during a session (maybe towards the end of the session or a round) ask for a show of hands from those who have not spoken today, or from those who have spoken only once, then allow those children a round (if they want one).

## Tension play

Once you have identified and mapped the ideas present that challenge one another (see *mapping* and *linking* in the Facilitation section, page 19) you can use these tensions to develop the enquiry in a number of ways. It can deepen the level of sophistication in the group as a whole; alternatively, it can require that a child improve their position as a result of defending it. It can also enliven an enquiry by allowing debates to unfold (see *mini debates* below).

## Mini debates

Occasionally, as with *tension play*, two children will lock horns and, as long as they do this respectfully, allow them a minute or two to respond to each other successively. This can benefit the session in a number of ways similar to those of *tension play*.

## Response detector

In order for **dialectic** to occur you will need to identify appropriate responses to ideas at the appropriate times. Although this should not be done all the time, as it will leave out many children, in order to encourage more dialectic it will sometimes be necessary, and very fruitful, to detect the responses to a particular idea. This distinguishes responses from those who have their own new ideas to offer; if you do this a few times successively, then this method can deepen thinking and reveal *thinking avenues* (see page 44).

## Talk Time and group work

Another strategy for speaker encouragement is Talk Time. This is a completely different dynamic in which some children will feel much more comfortable speaking. Once you have gone round and spoken with the quieter children, you can then encourage them to join in more during the enquiries by introducing their ideas into the discussion yourself, and then asking them to say more or to 'tell the class what you said to me'. Talk Time is mainly done in pairs but it does not really matter how many are talking with each other as long as everyone is talking with someone.

## Buzz

If the children become excited about an idea and start talking with each other when they shouldn't be (I call this 'buzz'), rather than fight them by trying to quieten them down, use this energy constructively and give them a minute or two of Talk Time. If they are over-excited about an idea, that is exactly what you want. Don't see the 'buzz' as something that needs to be subdued but as something to be channelled. In the martial art tai chi one is taught to use the opponent's energy against them rather than blocking it. You should not think of the children as opponents; you should think about how to use their energy positively so that it fuels the session rather than as something that should be suppressed.

## Group dynamics

I have identified two main dynamics in discussions, the second of which promotes sustained discussion sometimes allowing debates to continue without difficulty for an entire hour from one single question. They are the *Honeycomb Dynamic* and the *Web Dynamic*.

### The Honeycomb Dynamic

Here, the teacher maintains a tight control over the discussion by responding to and approving each contribution before moving on to the next speaker. This is a common response method from teachers in the classroom resulting in many single dialogues between the teacher and each child. This closes each contribution off, as if the children are in their own separate cell in a honeycomb, so that they are not linked to other contributions except in so far as the teacher decides to make links. In diagram form it might look something like this:

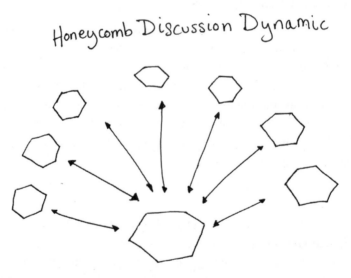

**Figure 4:** The Honeycomb Dynamic

The honeycomb dynamic is not the best way to spark a discussion or keep it moving; indeed, it can result in the teacher having to do a great deal of work in the discussion. An hour later the teacher will be very tired.

### The Web Dynamic

Even though the facilitator may still take the ball from each speaker before passing it on, they need not approve or respond to the speaker (except for echoing and clarifying). This leaves space for the responses of the children themselves. The facilitator looks for cues that suggest relevant responses such as a raised hand immediately after a point is made (or they may ask for raised hands only if they have something to say on the last point – see *Response detector*, page 25). This sort of dynamic fuels itself and the facilitator does a lot less work. They are simply blowing gently on the flames – the embers light each other. A web dynamic may look something like this:

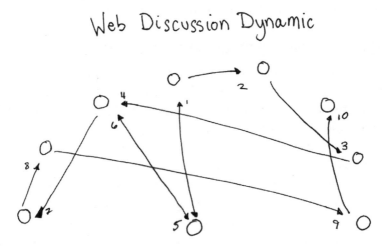

**Figure 5:** The Web Dynamic

Sometimes an enquiry may begin with something more like the honeycomb dynamic. This is not necessarily a bad thing as the children may be in some way inhibited but you certainly want to aim for the session to have more of a web dynamic as soon as you can.

## Self-management

One way for the facilitator to 'step out' of the group/discussion is for the group to learn how to self-manage. A clear and visible way for both yourself and the class to see this progress is the elimination of the ball. I have taken to spending 5–10 minutes allowing the children to self-manage without the ball in sessions with ages 9–11 depending on their level of maturity. What they should do is look for a natural space to make their contribution, while the others are asked to make way for the speaker and look for a natural space afterwards for *their* contribution. I have found that this method requires and encourages maturity from the group but, as with any speaker management method, it has its biases. For example, the more dominant and confident voices will be heard more often. It works very well in smaller groups with occasional promptings and guidance from the facilitator, but is difficult to sustain in a full class. I suggest not using it until the children are familiar with the usual 'ball' method.

You can also 'step out' of the discussion by sitting in the circle when someone starts speaking so the children stop addressing you and begin to address the group or child they are responding to. Once the enquiry has moved into a web dynamic this is easier to do. To encourage this I sometimes ask the speaker to address the group rather than me.

## Varying speaker management methods

Because all speaker management methods have their biases it is important to vary them. Therefore, every so often change from 'hands up' to 'no hands up' and *random selection*, making sure the selected child knows they do not have to speak. You may also find it useful to change the seating arrangement of the children so they are talking to people they wouldn't normally speak with during Talk Time. Unless you feel it would jeopardise the smooth running of the session, it can also be useful to get them to move around every time they do Talk Time to ensure they are talking to new people. One way of doing this is for every second child to move two seats away so that they are sitting next to a new person. Do make sure, however, that you leave them in their chosen seating arrangements from time to time, as they will often speak more naturally and easily with their friends. If you are worried about gender biases unconsciously creeping into your selection, then simply stick to a strict girl-then-boy rule whatever other speaker management method you are using. You may also find it useful to explicitly explain to the children some of your reasons for selection so they know why you are doing what you do (that they may have spoken more recently or more often than other children in the group). I say this because I have had reports from children that they do not like it when I look at them, then pass the ball to someone else. They can feel that you have decided you don't want to hear what they have to say. I have found that if you explain why you are doing this, they don't mind.

For an example session with suggestions of how to use Speaker Management methods see the companion website.

# Teaching Strategies

The Teaching Strategies will help you to understand the kind of thinking involved in philosophy, e.g. **critical thinking skills**. This part of the book will provide you with plenty of strategies for encouraging children to think in a more disciplined and methodical way without having to explicitly teach them critical thinking skills. This implicit approach and this kind of thinking can stay with students for the rest of their lives, and so I like to call these 'thinking habits' rather than thinking skills.

These strategies for teaching thinking in the classroom can be used in one's general teaching and are not limited just to philosophy sessions. I shall describe them each in general terms in the following pages, but each one will be given a context by way of an example in the sessions themselves. I have tried to find a place for each strategy somewhere in the book and for each session to demonstrate a different strategy. I suggest reading this part of the book before beginning the sessions, then I suggest re-reading the relevant strategies individually when you find them in the sessions.

**Figure 6:** The facilitator is like Ariadne, helping children to navigate their way around the maze of their own ideas.

In this book I have used the metaphor of *Theseus and the Labyrinth* from the Greek myth of *Theseus and the Minotaur* (see Teaching Strategy Box 'The labyrinth of thinking – anchoring and echoing', page 147). This metaphor illustrates that the role of the facilitator in aiding children's navigation around complex ideas is similar to the role of Princess Ariadne who provided Theseus with thread to help him find his way out of the labyrinth. The first two Teaching Strategies here (*anchoring* and *concept maps*) provide aid in navigation through the discussions.

# Anchor the children back to an idea or question

At university level students are told they should ask: 'Am I answering the question?' Making responses relevant is a discipline that can be learned at the very earliest stage of one's educational development. *Anchoring* means bringing the responses back to the Task Question. It can be done by simply re-asking the Task Question, being careful not to dismiss what has already been said. So, the *anchoring* is not a 'Yes, but …'; instead, it is a 'Yes, and …' You do not need to make explicit the irrelevance of a particular contribution; you just need to *anchor* them back to the Task Question. You may also find that by doing so they make explicit a link to the Task Question that was only implicit before and possibly too subtle for its relevance to be noticed by either you or the group. *Anchoring* deals well with irrelevant contributions but also reveals hidden relevance.

Thinking is all about making connections and, by anchoring the children back to the main question, you encourage them to make links between what they are saying and the main question. As I explained earlier, this can reveal a hidden relevance but there is a deeper reason why it's good to do this. What the children think about the Task Question will often be their *conclusion* and what they say will often be the supporting reasons, or *premises*, for the conclusion. So, by *anchoring* them back to the Task Question you require the children to link their idea to the conclusion which can lead them to formulating an *argument* (see *The Shadow of the Pyramid*, page 117 and Aristotle and the Logical Syllogism on the companion website). An example of this can be seen from a discussion with some children aged 10. The question being discussed was: 'Is $CO_2$ the same as air?' The children made many comments such as: 'Ingredients are in a cake but they are not the same thing as the cake', and: 'If we breathed in only $CO_2$ we would die'. By *anchoring* the children to the question 'Is $CO_2$ the same as air?', this encouraged them to show how what they had said either affirmed or denied the Task Question. One boy eventually said the following:

> 'If $CO_2$ is the same as air we should be able to breathe it in, because we breathe in air. But if we breathe in only $CO_2$ then we would die. So: $CO_2$ is not the same thing as air.'

The boy has expressed himself in argument form, with premises and a conclusion.

*Anchoring* is also useful for prompting children. So, if a child is chosen randomly (see *random selection* in the *Speaker Management* section, page 23), for instance, and they shrug their shoulders indicating they have nothing to say, try *anchoring* them to the Task Question before giving up. This removes the complexity of all the prior contributions that they may have heard and brings them straight back to the basic question about which they are much more likely to have something to say. If they still shrug their shoulders then move on.

## Anchoring segue: thinking is not remembering!

One very common response from children is: 'I forgot.' This can mean a number of things: it can mean they really have forgotten because they may have been waiting a long time for their turn to speak, but it can also be a way – especially with the younger children – of saying: 'I haven't got anything to say.' It is also sometimes linked with the fact that they might think there is a right answer that they haven't worked out. So, the expression 'I forgot' often needs to be dealt with. *Anchoring* is a good way of side-stepping the *I-forgot* problem. Just re-ask the Task Question and then add, 'What do you think about that?' The children need to learn that in an enquiry it's not about getting the 'right answer' and it's not about 'remembering answers', it's about '*thinking about whatever-it-is there and then*' and this can be done at any point in the discussion.

# Concept maps

These are also sometimes known as 'mind maps' and are particularly useful for helping children keep track of developing discussions, but these maps must be treated with caution. They are an aid to the enquiries rather than a central feature. It is the ideas of the children that a facilitator is interested in, so they should want to minimise any potential barrier between the discussion and the children's ideas. Procedures like *concept maps* can, if not treated properly, easily become barriers. I tend not to worry too much about neatness, grammar and punctuation – this is important only in so far as it should be intelligible. For ease, I avoid full sentences and stick to one or two key words for each idea wherever possible. *Concept maps* are used in a philosophy session to map the terrain already covered during the discussion so children can see at a glance what they have said and, roughly, how the ideas relate to each other. Another function of the *concept map* is to jot down questions that emerge during the enquiry. This performs two tasks: keeping a record of ideas for further enquiries; and helping to map the children's conceptual progress to keep them engaged. A sample *concept map* may look like this:

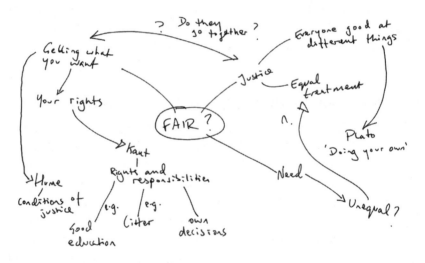

**Figure 7:** Concept Map example on the question 'What is fairness?'

# The 'imaginary disagreer'

Often during Talk Time, you will notice some of the children sitting in silence in their pairs. When you ask them why they are not talking they answer that they agree with each other. With this agreement their thinking ceases. To help the children re-engage in a debate you can ask them what they think someone might say if they disagreed with them. This is the *imaginary disagreer*. Of course, you can wait for someone else in the class to offer a challenge like this, but one important characteristic of philosophy is the silent dialogue method (see the online section *Can you do philosophy with children?*). The *imaginary disagreer* encourages children to adopt this method for themselves and thus removes the need for someone else to offer challenges to their own ideas. Sometimes I have found they agree with their *imaginary disagreer* and it causes them to change their mind. Use this technique frequently during Talk Time and occasionally during the enquiries if, for instance, you find unanimity among the class that brings the discussion to a halt.

# What's needed and what's enough?

In philosophy one of the concepts you will need to get to grips with when you begin your studies is that of 'necessary and sufficient conditions' – that is to say, the conditions under which something can be said to be true or present. This sounds daunting but one way of tackling it is to think of 'what is needed' (the necessary conditions) and 'what is enough' (the sufficient conditions). For instance, a square needs four sides, but this is not enough to guarantee that you have a square for the simple reason that four sides could also form a rhombus or a rectangle. The necessary and sufficient conditions for a square are as follows: a plain, closed, two-dimensional shape with four equal sides connected by right angles. The strategy is to take a concept or word such as 'square' and ask the children what is needed for a square. Answers can be listed under the concept-word on the board. Then ask the children when there is enough on the list so that they don't need to add anymore. It does not matter that they may not have reached an exhaustive list of necessary and sufficient conditions; that they are thinking in terms of necessary and sufficient reasons is reason enough to employ this strategy.

# Falsification and counter examples

If you ask children a question like 'Do you think everything changes and why?' you will often find they answer by providing an example that confirms their view: 'Yes, because when I grow up I change, I get taller and bigger.' This shows that 'some things change' but not that 'everything changes'. This is a common reasoning error in adults as well as children. We seek to confirm what we think is true but it would often be more fruitful to look for a refuting example rather than a confirming one. This habit of thinking is called *falsification* and is an incredibly useful habit to cultivate at a young age. When assessing a claim like 'everything changes' you only have to think of one example of something that does not change and the thesis collapses. The Task Question I would ask children when encouraging them to falsify in this instance is 'Can you think of something that does not change?' Or, to give another example, when assessing the claim that 'All birds fly' you might ask 'Can you think of a bird that doesn't fly?' rather than getting them to list all the birds that do fly. If they try to do the latter, they will be there rather a long time and will still have failed to prove that the claim is true. This strategy is worth bearing in mind whenever you try to prove or disprove a general claim that either you or somebody else has made. A refuting example is also known as a counter example. Children are often naturally very good at producing them. Once you've got one, the next question is: 'Is it a good counter example'?

# Break the circle

If you ask a child what 'growth' means, they will very often answer: 'It is when something grows.' Children naturally provide circular definitions (also known as tautological), and this activity is designed to encourage them to provide more informative answers. When you ask children to provide a definition of something or to say what something means simply add the stipulation that they must not say the word they are defining in their answer. For example: 'I want you to tell me what *thinking* is, but – here's the catch – you are not allowed to say the word *think* or *thinking* in your answer.' Write the word 'think' on the board, then write the phrase 'It is …' in the top left-hand corner; then encourage the children to begin their answers with 'It is …' to avoid them saying 'think' at the beginning of their answer. Write their ideas around the word 'think' using the *concept map* method (see page 31). When this has been done once or twice it can easily become a classroom habit; the children will soon start to say to each other that they are not allowed to say the word they are defining. For younger children you could make the words object-words rather than concept-words. Here is a suggested list of good *break the circle* words, though it can be done with any word.

- think
- try
- do
- mind
- love
- god

*Break the circle* is an excellent way of introducing enquiries into normal teaching. For instance, if you are using the topic of Martin Luther King to explore issues around freedom, then you could prelude your schemes of work with a *break the circle* on 'freedom'. *Break the circle* is an activity designed to encourage children to do what in philosophy is known as *conceptual analysis* (see the Philosophy Box on *conceptual analysis*, page 146).

# 'If the fact' and 'if the idea'

In discussions children often fall into debate about facts. Teachers often feel that in order to resolve an argument of this nature they need to know or find out what the facts are, but there is another way. Try to *if the fact*. Here 'if' has been turned into a verb. For example, imagine the children are discussing the question: 'Where would you be if you swapped brains with someone else?' It begins well but suddenly one of the children says that it's not possible to swap brains, then they simply argue about this fact following a 'yes-it-is, no-it-isn't' pattern. As a teacher you begin to panic because you don't know much about the science of brain transplantation, so your interesting discussion seems to have been hijacked. At this juncture you could say: 'We don't know much about whether it is true or not, but let's imagine for now that it could happen. *If* we *could* swap brains, where would you be if you swapped brains with someone else?' This kind of questioning will help to extricate a discussion from this factual cul-de-sac and allow it to continue in a conceptually informative way. The strategy also encourages children to think hypothetically – that is, in a 'what if?' way, which is a very important part of philosophical thinking. (See *The Ring of Gyges*, page 74 for an example of *if the fact*.)

A subtle variation on this is the related strategy *if the idea*. This invites children to test their idea by giving it a thinking context. It is different from *if the fact* only in that it deals with an idea rather than a fact. Other than that the strategy remains the same. (See *The Happy Prisoner*, page 93, for an example of *if the idea*.)

## The 'maybe' problem: if it, then anchor it, then open it up

Often when you ask younger children to respond to a scenario or thought experiment they begin their sentences with 'Maybe ...' then they construct an entire situation without any basis in the given scenario; they are continuing to write the story. For example, you may describe a situation where child A has lost something, say a toy, then sees child B with an identical toy. Child A then accuses child B of having stolen his toy. The Task Question at this point is: 'Does child A *know* that child B has stolen the item?' One of the children puts up their hand and says, 'Maybe they don't like each other and maybe he's trying to get him in to trouble.' Using the 'maybe' the child has introduced an element that is not in the story, and this threatens to send the children off-track so that they are not considering the relevant conceptual content: child A's knowledge of the situation. So, respond in kind and *if their idea* ('maybe' is a form of hypothetical thinking, so use an 'if' to continue the hypothetical thought), then *anchor* it back to the Task Question: 'So *if* that happened, do you think child A *knows* that child B stole his toy?' Using this strategy you do not need to tell the child they have missed the point and you do not need to struggle to get them to understand what it is you are asking; you simply redirect them with your questioning.

## Identify and challenge assumptions

Most statements assume something, though not all assumptions are significant enough to be challenged. For instance, this teaching strategy, *identify and challenge assumptions*, assumes that one *can* identify and challenge assumptions, and there are good reasons for thinking this is the case. However, assumptions are often important enough such that, if it turns out the assumption in question is unjustified or even false, then the whole case that rests on the assumption will collapse. Assumptions are rarely stated explicitly so it takes some skill and practice to spot them in the first place, let alone challenge them. Children often stumble upon an unstated assumption but they won't usually realise they have done that. Therefore, it is for the facilitator to make something of it when this happens. One useful way the facilitator can do this is to record questions as described in the *concept map* strategy as the children identify any assumptions. (See *The Prince and The Pig*, page 80.)

## Anchoring revisit: removing reintroduced concepts

A thought experiment attempts to remove irrelevant concepts and force our intuitions into a conceptual corner, but our instinct is to try to side-step this device. A thought experiment says, 'What if ...' and our instinct, especially if the scenario is unpalatable, is to say, 'But that wouldn't happen'. The philosopher then says, 'But what if it did?' In *Republic Island*, the Task Question asks: 'How do you deal with disagreements?' But the response 'We could continue until we agree' reintroduces the concept of 'agreeing', which the Task Question had removed, and this side-steps the question's force. However, it is perfectly conceivable, and it is a fact regarding human beings, that disagreements will occur, so it is still a perfectly good question to ask, 'How do we deal with disagreements?' This sort of thing happens a lot with children, so the strategy is simply to remove those assumptions by challenging them directly to consider the issue of the question or thought experiment. This does not have to be done aggressively. Here are some more examples of children reintroducing what the Task Question has attempted to remove.

Original Task Question A: *If you went to the edge of the universe, what would you find?*
Common response: 'You couldn't get there because you would run out of food.'
Original Task Question B: *If you could not get caught doing a crime, should you do it?*
Common response: 'You should not do it because they might have an alarm and then you might get caught.'

An *anchoring* technique combined with *if the idea* is required to bring children back to the relevant concepts and variables. You could respond to Task Question A with: 'If you *could* get to the edge of the universe, what do you think you would find? Would there be an edge or not?' And to B you could say: 'So let's imagine that there is *no way you could be caught*. Would it be okay to commit the crime then?' These questions have two parts structurally: the first half (the hypothetical element) emphasises the conditional situation; and the second half (the specificity element) pinpoints the question.

## Concept play

This strategy, together with *if the fact*, also deals with factual discussions with children, especially very young children, who are often in possession of very few facts. Allow the children to engage with factual discussions but from a conceptual point of view; allow them to consider 'what follows from what'.

For example, children can fruitfully discuss whether the mind and brain are the same thing or different without having to know much about the mind and brain. I asked some children aged 5–6 that very question. Some said the mind is *inside* the brain; a conceptual question on this would be: 'If the mind is inside the brain, is it the same or different?' Another child said: 'The mind is at the front of the head and the brain at the back, so they are different because they are in different places.' One young girl said: 'The mind is not *inside* the brain, it's part of it. The brain has lots of different parts that do different things and there is a *mind part*.' You can see from these examples that the factual accuracy is not so important here; what is of conceptual interest is the way the children are exploring how their idea of 'mind' *relates* to their idea of 'brain'. Once you know how to facilitate a discussion in a conceptual way it liberates you to be able to discuss just about anything. (See *Test the implications*, page 40 for how to manage this.)

# Multiple choices

One way to focus the discussion or provide what I call 'directions in thought' is to present a problem as a series of multiple choices. Be aware, though, that this may detract from the children's autonomy in the enquiries if done too much – but it does maintain choice while, at the same time, framing the discussion in a particular philosophical arena. This is one of the many ways in which a facilitator can help to maintain the balance between the children's autonomy and keeping it philosophical. (See *The Little Old Shop of Curiosities*, page 111.)

# Dissolving dichotomies

Very often discussions will begin dichotomously – in other words, children will often form two opposite positions in the class or group: one that affirms the question; and one that denies it. If you give children time to explore the issue, you will also discover they naturally find their way to alternative positions therefore dissolving the apparent dichotomy they began with. Expressions such as 'I think *yes* and *no*. *Yes* because … and *no* because …' indicate they have begun to recognise that there may be more to this question than simply A or B. Other expressions you may hear that indicate this are: 'Half and half', 'Sometimes A and sometimes B', 'I agree and disagree', 'In a sense A and in a sense B'. You can say the following to encourage children to think beyond a dichotomy: 'So, do you think A or do you think B? *Or, do you think something different?*'

# Primer discussions

These are simpler, but conceptually relevant, discussions that can be held before the introduction of a philosophical (or other difficult) idea. *Primer discussions* help to contextualise difficult or abstract ideas and also to make the ideas more accessible to more of the children. Used in normal teaching this is a learner-centred approach to the introduction of new material and is a good example of how enquiry can be used in the course of regular teaching. An enquiry around the question 'How long is a piece of string?', for instance, could be a good primer discussion for the introduction of the topic of measurement, quantity or number. (See *The Meaning of Ant Life*, page 57, and *The Shadow of the Pyramid*, page 117.)

# Second stage of stimulus: revealing controversies

Traditionally, methods of conducting philosophy discussions with children have often been understood as comprising two elements: 1) stimulus, and 2) response to stimulus. I would like to suggest a more complex way of understanding the stimulus aspect: 1) stimulus, 2) response to stimulus, and 3) using the response to the stimulus in 2 as a further stimulus for the enquiry by revealing controversies. Using this method one would introduce the stimulus (scenario or thought experiment etc.) in the usual way, then provide the Task Question followed by Talk Time. The facilitator then seeks to discover different positions to the Task Question (this can be done by talking with groups during Talk Time by inviting pairs (see *paired primer*, page 23) to share their ideas or just with *free play*). Those holding these positions are then invited to share their ideas with the group (note here that 'p' simply stands for 'whatever it is they don't think': A) 'I don't think that p because …' or: 'I do think that p because …' or: 'I think both because …' This method helps to reveal the controversies contained in the stimulus or Task Question.

Another common way that a controversy is revealed is when two speakers have the same reasons (x, y and z) but reach opposite conclusions ('p' and 'not p'): B) 'I do think that p because of x, y and z' and 'I don't think that p because of x, y and z.'

In A) the positions act as a stimulus by inviting the children to take one of these positions and to provide reasons for why they have done so; A) also challenges the group to think of any further positions there may be (see *Dissolving dichotomies*, page 38). B) is more subtle and challenges the children to consider which of the positions presented best follows from the reasons x, y and z as there is clearly a logical problem with opposite conclusions entailed by the same reasons. An even more subtle challenge offered by B) is for the group to identify that the reasons are in fact different when they appear the same – for instance, if an *equivocation* has occurred. An equivocation is when the two children have used the same word in their reasons but meant different things by them. An example would be when, in the same discussion, one person uses the word 'heart' to mean 'the organ which pumps blood around the body', while another uses 'heart' to mean 'our thoughts and feelings', but it is unclear that they mean quite different things.

The *paired primer* and the *mini dialogue* (see *Speaker Management*, page 23) are techniques designed to achieve the *revealing controversies* stage of the stimulus.

## Tension play

This strategy is closely related to *revealing controversies* but is different in that it is not part of the stimulus of the discussion, but is a technique to be used at any time during the discussion as a way of critically engaging the children with each others' ideas. *Tension play* is where ideas that have been introduced that have implicit tensions between them are brought out so that the tensions become explicit. For example, 'So, George, what do you think of Alice's earlier point that no one is really free?' This is a good method for engaging the children in a lively way and for developing philosophy using Hegelian dialectic methods (see Dialectic on the Companion Website).

## Test the implications

To elicit more from a child try putting the implications of their idea back to them for further consideration. Imagine a child says the following: 'Ceebie [a computer-robot] is not human because he does not have a brain.' The corresponding implication to this idea is: *humans must have a brain*. This implication, formulated as a question, would read as: 'Does that mean a human has to have a brain?'

This is a subtle introduction to argumentation. The implied argument is as follows.

Humans must have a brain.
Ceebie does not have a brain.
Therefore, Ceebie is not human.

In the following example the Task Question (TQ) links their idea and brings forth an implication that the child can then be encouraged to consider. The following example is taken from a session with some children aged 5–6.

---

TQ: Is the mind the same thing as the brain?
A (Child): The mind is inside the brain.
B (Facilitator): Does that mean that the mind is the same thing as the brain or different? (*Anchoring.*)
A: Different.
B: Why?
A: Because . . .

---

By using the implications of the children's ideas a facilitator can engage children with the argumentation process at a very early age without having to teach them formal argumentation. This involves the skilful use of a combined open-and-closed questioning technique. (See *Opening up closed questions* below and *The Ceebie Stories: The Android*, page 162 for an example of *test the implications*.) When using this strategy, or when questioning in general, it is very important to use a neutral tone rather than a rhetorical one (for instance, when you ask a seemingly innocent question in such a way that it implies you would be a fool to think it). To get an idea of this, practise speaking the following question with a variety of different tones to see how it changes the question's force: 'Does that mean a human has to have a brain?'

# Opening up closed questions

It is often said that teachers ask more closed questions than any other type of question, and it is commonly thought that this is a bad thing. Teachers are often told they need to ask more open questions to elicit more from the students. There is some truth in this but I think it is an over-simplification. Closed questions are necessary because they are the only kind of question that pinpoints responses to a specific area or answer and, as a teacher, it is often necessary to do this. Open questions are often too open-ended to be useful for what a teacher has to do: i.e. teach a specific fact or body of knowledge. I suggest it is okay to use closed questions but you should be aware of them and make sure that you open them up again to maintain an open-*ness* to the discussion. This keeps the overall flavour of the questioning and responses open, while retaining the benefit of the specificity of closed questioning. I call this an *open treatment* as distinct to *open questions*. Here is an example using the same discussion from the previous strategy.

---

TQ: Is the mind the same thing as the brain?
A (Child): The mind is *inside* the brain.
B (Facilitator): Does that mean that the mind is the same thing as the brain or different? (*Closed question.*)
A: Different.
B: Can you tell me why? (*Re-opens the questioning.*)
A: Because … (*Child goes on to explain themselves.*)

---

(See also *The Ceebie Stories: The Android*, page 162.)

# Either/or the if

This strategy is related to the *if the fact/idea* strategies but it makes use of another logical operation, the disjunctive, as well as the conditional ('if … then …') operation. The disjunctive takes the form: 'Either A or B'. Here's an example of how this teaching strategy was used with some 9 year-old children to allow for deeper hypothetical thinking, but also notice how it is used to diffuse a potentially awkward situation between a teacher, the group and a pupil. The Task Question was: 'Do unicorns have one horn or two?' Many in the class said that unicorns don't exist. The *if the fact* strategy was then used to surmount this possible obstacle to the discussion: '*If* they did exist, *then* how many horns would they have?' The enquiry continued until one child said: 'They do exist but you have to be lucky to see one.' Some of the other children immediately started to contest this child's view by repeating that they don't exist. The situation I found myself in, as a facilitator, was how to respond to the child. If I were to say that unicorns do not exist I would risk making them feel foolish, but if I said nothing then the other children would persist with their objections and this may also make the child feel foolish. So, on this occasion, I used the *either/or the if* strategy combined with the usual *anchoring* technique. I began by saying: 'Let's think about it both ways. If they *did* exist, then how many horns would they have and how would you find out?' Then I asked, 'If they *didn't* exist, then how many horns would they have?'

# The web of understanding

When you are trying to explain something to the class, usually the biggest problem is trying to get everyone to understand. This can be frustrating, especially if you find yourself repeating something over and over but to no avail. In this instance, try altering your strategy: instead of trying to explain the idea to the class, *get the members of the class to explain the idea to each other*. Find someone who understands the idea and ask them to explain it in their own words. If necessary ask them to try again using different words. Once someone else understands, ask them to explain it in their own words. You should soon start to see understanding spread throughout the classroom as the class self-facilitates its understanding. This is invariably more successful than trying to explain it yourself, as children naturally use the same register of language with each other. It is advisable to note the language and concepts they use so that you can revise how you present the material next time or even how you present the next stage of the same material.

# Adopting 'voices'

Although you are encouraged not to express your own opinions in these sessions and not to challenge the children personally, there are some appropriate ways that you can do this. Adopting voices can be a very useful way to engage and challenge children and bring in new ideas.

You can use the *voice of a philosopher/character*. This involves role-playing as a philosopher/character, so that you can use the opportunity to try to persuade the children of a particular idea in order to engage them more fully with the argument. In order to do this you need to be confident that you understand the idea yourself so that you can speak on the philosopher's behalf without misrepresenting them. If you are unsure about the extent to which you can do this then it is best to avoid it. This is not an opportunity for you to express your own ideas, only those of the philosopher or character in the session, so make sure you reiterate whose *voice* you are using. For example, 'Socrates would say that you can only be happy if you do good.' (See *The Ring of Gyges*, page 74.)

You can also use the *voice of a peer*. When you have run a few sessions, and especially if you are keeping good records of the sessions, then it can be fruitful to use some of the insights from other sessions to challenge or engage the children during an Enquiry. This is especially useful if the children are hovering over an interesting or philosophical insight that they are not quite getting to but that you know other classes of a similar age have reached.

# Thinking avenues and the response detectors

Using traditional methods of Speaker Management, such as 'opportunity for all' or 'hands up', can mean that good dialectical discussions are lost, as those with responses don't get a chance to speak until their response is 'out of date' and no longer has a context, or until the children have forgotten their response. During the discussion there will be times when you want to detect what I call 'thinking avenues'. These are connected lines of thought or reasoning from multiple participants. Naturally, you will want to follow them and develop them. This benefits the group, as well as those taking part, because the discussion can then be more easily brought to a new level of depth or sophistication and this will often carry the other group members with it to the new level.

Finding thinking avenues can be done by using a *response detector*. One way to detect responses is to ask for 'only hands of those with something to say about the last point(s)'. Another, slightly more sophisticated method, is for them to use different hand signals to indicate what kind of comment they have: a full hand for a new idea or one finger for a response to a previous idea. The latter method requires that children are able to classify their own contributions, but giving them the responsibility of doing this is an excellent way for them to develop this skill. Using *response detectors* should be selective, returning to other Speaker Management methods so that others can join in. Use them when you hear something of philosophical importance in the enquiry or if you sense the group is instantly stimulated by an idea (body language such as hands shooting up usually gives you the best indication that this has happened). *Response detectors* can also be used to detect responses to successive ideas following the *thinking avenue* for several steps before returning to the group as a whole.

# *Sine qua non*: the essence of a thing

*Sine qua non* is a Latin term that literally means 'without which not'. In English, this means the essential feature without which you would no longer have a particular concept. So, if you had a 'red square', what feature(s) are so essential to it for it to be a square, such that, if you removed it (or them) it would no longer be a square? The feature of 'being red' is not essential, as a square that is not red is still a square. The feature of 'having right angles', however, is essential, as a square with no right angles could no longer be a square. In short, the strategy of *sine qua non* invites thinkers to find the essential features of a thing. For instance, can you think of some feature or quality of yourself that is so important to your identity, that, without it, you would no longer be you? (See *Where Are You?*, page 182.)

# Sympathise and criticise the philosopher/idea

If an idea is introduced, then it can sometimes be useful to begin by trying to think why the philosopher or child thought what they did. This involves an element of sympathising with the idea. Once this has been done, we can then think about what is wrong with the idea. This encourages the habit of a balanced view from the children when considering ideas. It is related to *either/or the if* strategy, because the children are thinking about a theory or idea both ways: A) 'If it is right then why would it be right?', and B) 'If it is wrong then why would it be wrong?' (See *Get Stuffed: Fun with Metaphysics*, on page 186.)

# Section 2:
## The PhiE Sessions

# The Chair

*This session is dedicated to Rokas and Keeley from the after-school club at Hither Green School*

Suitable for age 7 and upwards.
Star rating: **

## Themes

Things and what they are to us
Perception
Points of view
Names and referring terms

## Philosophy

'Philosophy begins in wonder.' **Plato**
'Philosophy is looking beyond what you see.' Year 9 pupil

This session is designed to engage the children with a philosophical process, with the act of philosophising in contrast to learning about philosophy. In other words, they are learning to do philosophy straight away. *The Chair* has been written in sections, each of which have a stimulus followed by Talk Time and an enquiry.

This session is an excellent introduction to children doing philosophy for the first time and is one I have run successfully with age 7 and upwards, simplifying it accordingly. I often explain that what we do in philosophy is take what seems obvious (like 'This is a chair!'), then think about it more deeply to discover all the further possibilities that may lie hidden (such as 'It's nothing!' or 'It is anything you want it to be' or 'It is everything' etc.). I like to quote one pupil who said that philosophy is about 'looking beyond what you see'. This short explanation does two important things: it shows philosophy's *exploratory* quality and also its *transformative* quality. That is to say, it shows how thinking about something can change our view of what it is without physically changing it. A chair can transform from something banal and uninteresting to something fresh with exciting new possibilities and therefore become worth spending at least an hour thinking and talking about. I like to think that philosophy has an alchemical power and, just as the alchemists of old believed that one could change base metals into gold, the philosopher has the power to change the banal into something sparkling with interest, reawakening a wonder about things towards which wonder may have been lost, even for the teacher too.

Make sure that, if you decide to say any of this by way of an introduction to philosophy, you should say it at the end of the session, when the children have done their philosophising, so that you are describing what they have already done rather than telling them what they should do.

# Stimulus

Place a chair in the centre of the room so that everyone can see. Ask the children: 'What is this?' The expected answer is: 'A chair.' Then say, 'Let's see what you think by the end of the session, shall we?' Tell the following story.

## Part one

*I want you to imagine a room with many windows, brightly lit by the sun, with an object in it, much like this. [Point to the chair.] During the day a man walks in and sees the object. He thinks, 'Ah, somewhere to sit down', and he sits and rests for a time because he has been on his feet for most of the day. After a while he looks at his watch and hurries out of the room. Later that day, a dog comes into the room. The dog sees the object and sits under it to get some shade from the sun – for it is a hot day. The dog stays there for a while, panting, then it trots off.*

*So, the man thought the object was something to sit on and the dog thought it was shelter from the sun.*

> TQ 1: What is this object? Something to sit on or something to shelter under? Or is it something else?

This is a good time to stop for discussion. Use a *concept map* to keep track of the children's ideas. When the discussion has run for about 10 minutes move on to the next part of the story.

---

**Teaching Strategy: concept maps (page 31)**

Concept maps help both the teacher and children to keep track of what has been said during a discussion. Use key words and avoid sentences where possible so that the focus is on the discussion and not what's been written on the board. Use the concept map to show links between ideas and make tensions visible. This is one of the key Ariadne-like tools for helping children navigate their way through discussions while keeping track of what has already been said. It helps to cultivate a holistic view of an enquiry so that one is aware of what has been said, what is being said and what could be said in light of the former two. (For a sample concept map see page 32.)

---

## Part two

*Later that night, when nobody else is around, an alien spaceship lands and out of it come some aliens that are zooming around the galaxy collecting objects from different planets. From this planet they collect this object [point to the chair]. They take it back to the ship and then, in a blink, the ship silently vanishes back into outer space at light speed. On board the ship the aliens study the object, trying to work out what it is. They have no idea.*

TQ 2: If the aliens do not know what the object is, then what is it?

This is an optional discussion point. If time is short then skip it. However, you may want to return to it later to refer to the idea that 'knowing' is important when trying to say what makes something what it is.

## Part three

*These particular Aliens are different from humans but in some ways similar: they have heads and arms and legs, but they have two arms on each side and three legs. They only have one head, but it is bigger and squarer than a human head. They discover that the object they took fits on their heads perfectly and they decide that it must be a hat. They gaze at themselves and think they look magnificent with the new hat placed on their heads. When they return to their planet, Zargon, all the other aliens are very impressed with the new alien headgear. The alien that took the object in the first place, Zarboog, then has an idea. Zarboog has thousands of the 'hats' made to sell them to other aliens.*

TQ 3: What is the object now? A chair, a shelter, a hat or something else?

Follow this with more Talk Time and enquiry. In order for the session to flow, you may decide to dispense with Talk Time after some of the Task Questions and simply allow the enquiry to continue.

## Part four

*Hundreds of years pass. Humans have now mastered interstellar space flight. By this time, chairs have no legs and float around so that people don't have to get out of them. One day, humans arrive at the planet Zargon. They make contact with the aliens, become friends and learn their language. When the time comes for them to leave, the aliens present them with a parting gift: one of their still very fashionable hats [point to the chair]. The humans are delighted and zoom back to Earth with the alien gift. When they return to Earth they announce that they have made alien contact and they hand over the gift to a space museum. It is placed in a special display case and underneath the object is written: 'Zargonian hat'.*

TQ 4: Is the object a Zargonian hat?

Possibly allow more Talk Time and enquiry.

## Part five

*Back on Zargon, the original object brought back by Zarboog has been passed down to Zarboog's offspring and now occupies pride of place in Zarboog's great, great grandson's house, Zarboog III. It is very valuable and is heavily protected with alarms. One night there is a burglary and the object is stolen. The thieves fly off into space with the stolen object but with the Zargonian-police right behind them. There is a space battle and the thieves' spaceship is destroyed. The object flies through space and lands on a passing asteroid upside down. It is carried off into deep space and lost.*

*The asteroid floats through space for ten years, then hundreds of years, then thousands of years, then millions of years and, finally, billions of years. There are no longer any Zargonians or humans left; they have all long since perished.*

> TQ 5: What is the object now that there are no humans or Zargonians (or anything else) to see it or use it?

Allow more Talk Time and enquiry. You may need to *anchor* (see Teaching Strategy box) the children by reminding them that there really is nothing left to be able to see it or use it.

## Part six

*When the object fell to the asteroid, it landed upside down. Underneath, clearly written at the time of its manufacture on Earth, it says, 'chair'.*

> TQ 6: Does this mean that the object was just a chair all along?

To help keep the pace up of this session it is a good idea to manage your time. Perhaps give the group 10 minutes with each part. Play this by ear and do not artificially bring a vigorous discussion to a close just to meet your time-keeping requirements. Remember: this session can be extended over two or even three lessons. If you are only going to run this for one session, then it is important to make sure that, no matter what you leave out, you do include the climax (the asteroid part at the end) for the reasons I list below. Keep in mind the *Extension Activity* ideas I have included at the end of the session to bring into the enquiry when you see an opportunity, though only where there is an opportunity. You must not, at any point in this session, refer to the chair as 'a chair'; refer to it only as 'the object' or 'this object'. This may be a little difficult at first but it is essential when asking the question 'What is it?' that you do not answer the question by calling it a 'chair'. There is a sense in which the expression 'this object' also answers the question, but it is the most neutral expression short of not referring to it at all, which would make the session very difficult.

---

🎓   **Teaching Strategy: Anchoring (page 30)**

To maintain the focus of this session it is important to use the *anchoring* technique throughout, asking the children, 'So, what is it then?' *Anchoring* helps to:

- keep things relevant and focused
- reveal hidden relevance
- link ideas to the task question
- produce arguments
- clarify and prompt thinking.

---

It is important to reach the 'asteroid' section of the story (Part Five) because most children define or attempt to understand what the chair is in relation to a perceiver, usually themselves. The first aim of this exercise is for them to move beyond themselves to consider the object from other points of view (e.g. a dog and then an alien). The next phase is to invite the children to consider what the object would be when it is removed entirely from a perceiver of any kind. This is a version of the well-known philosophical question 'If a tree falls in a forest and there is no one around to hear it, does it make a sound?' It is, however, more difficult for the children to see the point of this question if they jump straight in with it. The preamble to this story prepares them for this question and by the time you reach the climax of the story (the 'asteroid' section) they will be well primed for tackling this strange question and better placed to understand it. This is an example of the use of a *primer discussion* (see page 39 and *The Meaning of Ant Life*, on page 57).

---

🔍   **Extension activities**

Further ideas that have cropped up during discussions and which can be inserted at appropriate times according to ideas that the children introduce are as follows.

### Copying

What would happen if it turned out that we had not designed it in the first place but had copied it from something left by other aliens or had simply used it after it had been left behind on Earth? Would that mean that it was not really a chair?

---

### A paradox

A more complex version of this that emerged from one session was that the aliens were time-travelling aliens that took the original 'chair' they had found on Earth and travelled back in time to introduce it to humans, thus creating a paradoxical situation where the aliens had found it from the humans but the humans had also found it from the aliens! *What would it be then?*

### Two chairs

Occasionally, I put two 'chairs' in the middle of the room and then state that one of them was made on Earth by humans to be a chair and the other was made by aliens to be a hat, but we don't know which is which. So, the question might then be: How could we tell the difference? Or: Would they be different things?

### How many things in the room?

Another situation is to ask the children to imagine a dog, a human and an alien all standing in a room together looking at the 'chair'. They all think it is a different thing: a shelter for the dog, a chair for the human and a hat for the alien. So, not counting the dog, the human or the alien, does this mean that there are three things in the room or just one? A good follow-up question to this is: How many things would there be if they all left the room?

# Online

Main philosophy:
Berkeley and Idealism
Kant and the 'Thing In Itself'

Related philosophy:
Aristotle and Teleology
Hobbes and Materialism
Metaphysics: What There Is

**Related Sessions**

The Meaning of Ant Life (page 57)
Can You Step in the Same River Twice (page 61)
The Ship of Theseus (page 86)
Thinking About Nothing (page 135)
Get Stuffed: Fun with Metaphysics (page 186)

# The Meaning of Ant Life

*This session is dedicated to the children of Rathfern Primary School.*

Suitable for age 9 and upwards.
Star rating: **

## Themes

Purpose and design
Existentialism
God and religion
Value

## Philosophy

This session asks the big question 'What's it all about?' If you are considering something's purpose or design, then in philosophy this is known as teleology (from the Ancient Greek *telos*, meaning design or purpose). To get an idea of what this means consider the following.

TQ 1: What are these things for?
A chair.
A tree.
A person.

These things each engender a very different kind of answer. The question of meaning in life leads one to consider what we are here for. But giving a purpose to something like a life form such as a human being can seem parochial, and *The Meaning of Ant Life* illustrates the problem with parochial answers to this question. This session works quite well as a follow-up to *The Chair*, as the sorts of things discussed in that session lead naturally to issues connected with this one. Also, if you use TQ/1 before you read the story you will provide the children with a natural segue into this session, as it begins with a chair (see the teaching strategy *primer discussions* in this session and on page 39).

# Stimulus

*There was once a colony of ants. One day, the ants were discussing what it's all about.*

*'Why are we here?' they had said. 'What are here for?'*

*Some said they were here to work hard and provide for the colony; others said they were here to make more ants to keep the species going; others suggested that perhaps they were here to enjoy themselves, but then pointed out that ants aren't particularly good at that; others said they are here not for their own benefit but for the benefit of the colony as a whole ... The discussion went on and on into the night. The ants simply could not decide on one reason why they were here on the earth.*

*The very next day an explorer ant returned from a big adventure: he had been exploring the big, wide world. His return was celebrated by the whole colony, as they had not seen him for a long time and it had been widely supposed, among the colony, that he must have perished on his journey. Everyone wanted to know what he had seen on his adventures.*

*When he heard what it was the ants had been arguing about all night, he gathered them all around him and announced the following:*

*'As you all know, I have been around the world and seen things that the rest of you have never seen and probably never will see. I've seen waterfalls glistening with rainbows in the sun; I've seen enormous structures reaching up to the heavens with giant two-legged ants scurrying around them like termites.'*

*The other ants gasped at the terrifying idea of giant termites. The explorer ant continued:*

*'I have learned things that none of you know. I've learned about planets and the history of the world; I've learned all about the many other animals that live in the world and have lived in the world but are no more. And I think I am now in a position to answer your question: "Why are we here?"'*

*All the ants leaned forward in anticipation of his answer.*

'We are here ...', he paused and then lowered his voice to no more than a whisper, 'to provide food for anteaters. That's it!' He exclaimed much more loudly, 'We are food for ant-eaters.' The colony looked at him in shocked amazement.

'Think about it,' he went on. 'They are perfectly designed for eating us and we are perfectly designed to be eaten by them; they have long sticky tongues for reaching into our nests and we easily stick to sticky things; they have thick fur so that we can't bite them. So, there it is: we must be here to be food for anteaters.'

*This big revelation set the ants arguing about this for so long, they are still arguing about it to this day.*

TQ 2: What do you think of the explorer-ant's big revelation? Is he right? Are ants just food for anteaters?

Nested Questions
- Are we here for a specific reason or no reasons or something else?
- Do we put meaning into our lives or do we need something external to confer meaning to our lives?
- What is meaning?

## Teaching Strategy: Primer discussions (page 39)

Sometimes it is better to start with a stimulus, then allow the discussion to unfold, such as with *The Chair* (page 47) session and *The Ship of Theseus* (page 86), but other sessions seem to work better with a conceptual discussion before the introduction of the stimulus such as with *The Shadow of the Pyramid* (page 117) and *The Meaning of Ant Life* (page 57). It can help to focus the philosophical material within the stimulus, but it can also allow the children to flex their conceptual muscles, as it were, before considering the related concepts that lie within the story. You will be surprised by the complexity of ideas and material that the children can deal with if you prime them in the right way. Contrast this with the sheer consternation you will be met with if you just plonk a complex philosophical idea in front of them with no prior contextualisation. Simply asking the question 'How big is big?' before the *The Shadow of the Pyramid* (see page 117) makes a huge difference. The priming question does not need to be – and in fact benefits from not being – complicated, as long as it is conceptually relevant and rich. In this session the priming question is *What are things for?* in the context of considering starkly different kinds of things: a chair, a tree and a person.

# Online

Main philosophy:
Aristotle and Teleology

Related philosophy:
Mill and Utilitarianism
Socrates, Aristotle and the Soul
Sartre, de Beauvoir and Human Nature

---

 **Related sessions**

The Chair (page 49)
The Prince and the Pig (page 80)
The Happy Prisoner (page 93)
Goldfinger (page 98)

# Can You Step in the Same River Twice?

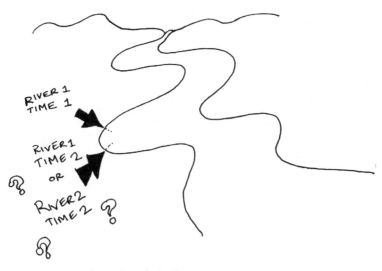

Is it the same river as it flows through time?

*This is dedicated to the children of St. Mary's Primary School, Lewisham.*

Suitable for age 8 and upwards.
Star rating: *

## Themes

Change
Arguments
Identity
Necessary and sufficient conditions
Rivers and water cycles

# Philosophy

This is one of the most famous philosophical questions and is thought to have been first asked by Heraclitus of Ephesus (fl. c. 500 BCE). As with *The Ship of Theseus* session (page 86), this session deals with change and identity. These are two of the most approachable philosophical themes for children, as there is a sense in which they have already had to grapple with a philosophical problem: they see the world in absolute, static entities ('good and bad', 'right and wrong', 'me and you') but they *experience* the world as changing. So, here we have a philosophical problem with which the children may already be acquainted.

# Stimulus

*Timmy and Tina have gone to a river with their parents for a picnic. They are paddling in the river close to the riverbank swishing their fishing nets around trying to catch tadpoles. They also play 'Pooh-sticks', the famous game played by Winnie-the-Pooh. (Timmy and Tina both drop a stick into the river from one side of a bridge and then race to the other side to see which one emerges first.) After a while, their mum calls for them to come and eat their sandwiches. They run up to their picnic rug and sit down to tuck into their lunch. Later, when they have finished eating Timmy says, 'I'm going back down to the river to catch some more tadpoles.'*

*Tina looks at him and says, 'Which river?'*

*Timmy is a little puzzled by her question and says, 'The same one we were in earlier. Which one did you think?' he asks sarcastically, 'There's only one river around here.'*

*His sister thinks for a moment and then looks at him with a cheeky smile and says, 'But it's not the same river. You can't step in the same river twice because when you get there it will be a different river.'*

> TQ: Can you say why Tina thinks it is a different river?

Give the children Talk Time in pairs and find out what they think. If they are not having the Heraclitean insight that it is 'not the same river because the water is constantly flowing', then you could present an argument between the two characters to bring this out, though I suggest resisting this unless you have to. Get the children to assess the arguments' merits and demerits by simply asking them who they agree with and why.

'What do you mean?' asks the puzzled Timmy.

'It won't be the same river because the water that was there when we were there last will have flowed away. The river has changed so it's not the same river, it's a different one.' Tina stands looking at Timmy with her arms crossed waiting for an answer.

'Oh, I get what you mean now,' says Timmy, 'but it's still the same river only with different water.'

He sister glares at him. 'That's all a river is though: water,' she says. 'So, if the water has moved, then it's a different river, surely?'

One strategy following this reading is to get children into pairs and ask them to adopt either Timmy's or Tina's position, then discuss with each other from that point of view, trying to persuade the other one of their position. Follow this with an enquiry.

### Teaching Strategy: What's needed and what's enough? (page 33)

One line of inquiry following this is to explore with the children what makes a river. Do a *what's needed and what's enough?* strategy with them on 'What is a river?' Write the word 'river' on the board, then set the task of listing all the features a river would need to be a river. It might look like this.

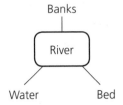

At each point ask the children if they can think of an example of a river without the relevant feature. For instance, you might not need 'water' for a river because you could have a river of lava, chocolate or mercury. So, what does it need? 'Water' could be replaced with 'a liquid', but then the next question is 'could you have a dry river?' If there is no water or any other flowing substance in the river, is it still a river? Do not expect this kind of discussion to be concluded. The fact that the children are engaging with this kind of thinking is valuable enough.

# Everything changes

The next stage of this session is to introduce the children to Heraclitus and explain that this question, *Can you step in the same river twice?*, comes from Heraclitus who asked the question two and a half thousand years ago (see the companion website for more on Heraclitus). Write his name on the board, then explain that he also thought that 'everything changes'. Write this phrase on the board, then ask the children: 'If Heraclitus thought that everything changes, what do you think his answer to the question *Can you step in the same river twice?* would be?' This is encouraging them to think in argument form. Below is an example of an argument that you may detect in some of the answers.

> If Heraclitus believes that everything changes, then he must think that rivers also change.
>
> If rivers also change, then you cannot step in the same river twice because it is always changing.
>
> So, his answer must be: 'No, you cannot step in the same river twice.'

This is historically probably what Heraclitus thought, but some children may feel that though a river always changes there is a sense in which it remains the same thing. So, for these children it will not follow that if rivers change then you cannot step in the same river.

Even though there is an answer here, historically it is still contentious what the answer is, so avoid providing one or making it clear that you expect one. Simply allow the children to think this through together, whatever it is they conclude. You could encourage them to respond to each other and thereby facilitate each other's understanding, but try to avoid the 'guess-what's-in-my-head' teaching here. Do not spend too long on this.

 **Teaching Strategy: Falsification and counter examples (page 33)**

Now ask the children if they agree with Heraclitus that 'everything changes'. Follow this with Talk Time and an enquiry, then set a further Task Question designed to encourage them to falsify the hypothesis: 'Can you think of something that doesn't change?' Give them more Talk Time and another enquiry. I have had these suggestions: 'the past'; 'numbers'; 'a book in a box on the moon'; 'your name'; 'God' and 'an event'. If they do this then they will have come up with what is known as a *counter-example* – that is, an example that goes counter to the claim.

### Philosophy: Writing philosophy

If you want to encourage children to write philosophy, then provide them with a 'philosophy journal' or a philosophy homework sheet and set them the Task Question that has been discussed in the session or an appropriate **Set Question**. The session then acts as a *primer discussion* that should help them unlock their ideas about the topic, which, in turn, should yield more ideas in any work they do.

# Online

Main philosophy:
Heraclitus and Change

Related philosophy:
Aristotle and the Logical Syllogism
Berkeley and Idealism
Hobbes and Materialism
Leibniz and Identity
St. Augustine and Time
The Pre-Socratics and Natural Philosophy
Metaphysics: What There Is

### Related Sessions

The Chair (page 49)
The Ship of Theseus (page 86)
The Ceebie Stories: The Rebuild (page 172)
Where Are You? (page 182)
Get Stuffed: Fun with Metaphysics (page 186)

# Republic Island

How would *you* survive?

*This session is dedicated to the 2008 Year 2 class at Brindishe Primary School, Lewisham.*

Suitable for age 7 and upwards.
Star rating: *

## Themes

Group decision-making
Politics
Fairness
Rules
Society
Citizenship
Islands

# Philosophy

These sessions are based on Plato's dialogue *The Republic* in which Plato explores the question of what justice is, then attempts to construct the ideal state based on the conclusions he reaches in his discussions. It is one of the most talked about books of political philosophy and possibly the most famous book of philosophy ever written.

The objectives of these sessions are for children to engage with decision-making without the help of adults in order for them to consider the nature of 'what is right' in groups or society. Though we might call this principle 'justice', as translations of Plato do, with children it is easier to use the word 'fair' in its place. They will also learn some important social skills particularly how to deal with disagreements among themselves and they will explore some of their justifications for these methods. The various concepts of justice (or 'fairness') that often emerge are: justice as 'getting what you want'; justice as 'equal share'; justice as 'equal treatment'; justice as 'need'; justice as 'priority'; justice as 'strength'; and possibly justice as something that is 'sensitive to changing situations'. There may be others but these are the most common conceptions of justice/fairness that are likely to crop up. One question to bear in mind when exploring these ideas is 'do these concepts go together?' For instance, does the conception of fairness as 'getting what you want' sit comfortably with justice as 'equal share'? If everyone got what they wanted would they have an equal share? And likewise, does 'need' go with 'equal treatment'?

Unlike many of the other PhiE sessions, *Republic Island* covers a number of parts. One simple way of approaching this is to make each part a session. I usually make the first two parts, *Surviving* and *Making Decisions*, one session and then the next two parts, *The Rules* and *What is Fair?* into one session.

# Stimulus

## Part one: Surviving as a castaway

*Imagine you are travelling across the Pacific Ocean at about the time of the ancient Greeks, which means there is no electricity or machines. Your transport is a large wooden ship with huge sails that has been travelling for weeks across a featureless sea. A darkly powerful storm whips up and rages for days. The storm eventually capsizes your ship and you find yourself tossed about by the high waves. You manage to grab hold of a free-floating piece of wood, such as a part of the mast or a chest, and you hang onto it for your life.*

*The following morning the storm has subsided and you find that you have been washed up on the beach of a tropical island. The sun is shining and the weather is beautifully calm. You stand up and decide to explore the island, which will be your home for the foreseeable future.*

*You discover that this island is not inhabited and seems never to have been. There is absolutely no sign of human life whatsoever. All around the perimeter is a golden sandy beach. The middle of the island is covered with a lush forest full of animals and different fruits. There is a mountain at the heart of the forest from which run several fresh water streams that form a lake at the bottom, full of fish. There is plenty here for you to live on.*

*When you have returned from your exploration of the island you find that there are some other survivors from the wrecked ship, four in total. You gather together and discuss what you should do. Your first task is to do your best to survive on your newly found home.*

> TQ 1: How would you survive?

This task can be done in groups (see below) with Talk Time, or you can simply perform it together as a class taking as long as you deem necessary. Many activities could be introduced to extend this part (see below for Extension Activity suggestions). From the point of view of engaging in a philosophical enquiry you would not want to spend too long on this part of the task. 10 minutes would be sufficient.

## Extension Activities

- Children could draw maps of their island making sure it includes the features described.
- Tell or read them the story of *Robinson Crusoe* by Daniel Defoe. Ask them to imagine the scenario, but with them alone. Possible Task Questions: 'Would you be able to be happy alone?', 'Would you need words or language if you lived alone?', 'Do you need to worry about being good and following rules if you are completely alone?', 'Can you think of a rule that you would still need to live by if you were alone on an island?'
- Watch the film *Castaway* (or an extract of it) starring Tom Hanks. (This will depend on the age group of the class.) Draw the children's attention to any similarities between their own suggestions and the decisions made by Tom Hank's character (it is important to do the activity before you show the film so as not to influence their own thinking during the task).

# Part two: Making decisions

For this part, children should be split into groups, with each group comprising the five survivors on the island. (Remind them that the different groups will not be on the same island, so the groups cannot confer with or help each other.) To select the groups, and also to introduce a random element to them, I suggest the following method: count around the class giving each child a number from 1 to 5. Ask each child to hold up the requisite number of fingers to signify their designated number, so: 1 finger is held up for children in group number 1, and 2 fingers for children in group number 2 etc. This avoids you or the children having to remember who is in which group. Ask all the children with the same number to sit together. Now the entire class should be in their respective groups appropriately spaced away from each other. Explain that if they really were shipwrecked they would not be able to choose who their fellow survivors would be. (You may want to make a few executive swaps if you see some potential problems with certain children being together.)

Describe their homes and general dwelling place with all the various amenities they thought of in Part one. Then ask them to think of a name for their new 'town-of-five'. It is important not to advise them on how to do this. If they ask for help, then role-play your way out of it: 'I am not really here: all the teachers and adults were lost with the ship, so you'll have to do this without any help.' Of course, you are there to intervene if really necessary (if there are real tears, for instance), but you will aim to minimise your presence, so that they are thinking for themselves about how to best achieve this task. Set them a time limit, though you may decide to stop when they all seem ready.

Now ask them (and write on the board) the following questions.

- Did you find a name for your island?
- How did you decide?
- Did you have any problems deciding?
- How did you/can you solve the problems? (Encourage the class to work together to answer this question.

Ask each group each of these questions, and list the names and the methods with which they decided on their names. You may expect responses such as:

- agreement
- vote
- lottery of some kind
- leader's decision etc.

You should encourage a critical evaluation of the methods. One way to do this is to ask any children who complain that it wasn't fair why they think it wasn't fair. Another way is to invite them to answer TQ 2.

> TQ 2 Which do the children think is the best method and why?

One interesting tension that often crops up is that children will often decide that voting is the best system (especially currently with all the vote-based programmes they see on television). But if the vote is not unanimous, then they will abandon it and move to another name. So, even though they understand the importance of everyone having a voice in the voting system, they do not always grasp how a vote is supposed to deal with disagreement. A good question to help them explore this is: 'So, is voting only fair when everyone agrees?' Notice that the word 'fair' is present already. A good TQ for this section is given below.

> TQ 3: If you have disagreements in your town how would you deal with it?

 **Teaching Strategy: Removing reintroduced concepts (page 36)**

TQ 2 eliminates the 'agreement' method, where the children simply find a name they all agree on. However, they may try to reintroduce this element by answering the Task Question as follows: 'We will find a name we all agree on.' It is okay, in this situation, to explicitly remove the agreement element, as it would defeat the object to leave it in: 'But if you still disagreed what would you do?' Gently *anchor* them back to this until they consider the issue of how to deal with disagreement.

## Part three: The rules

Once the children have learned to survive and have named their new town, the next important stage is to decide what rules they should have, or whether they think they should have any at all. Give them plenty of time to talk this through in their groups or as a class. This section should be concept-mapped, so everyone can see how the discussion has proceeded. One really good Task Question that may find its way in via one of the children, or, if not, would be fine for you to introduce is given below.

TQ 4: Should we have the rule that 'there should be no rules'?

This section may include a discussion of who should rule and why. Should it be the strongest? The wisest? Everybody? Nobody? Who? This would make a good Task Question.

TQ 5: Who should rule? And why?

---

### Extension Activity: Rawls' rules

Try the following activity based on John Rawls' 'veil of ignorance' thought experiment: ask the children to come up with a list of school rules where they don't know if they would be the head teacher, a teacher, a pupil, a top-set student, a bottom-set student, and where they don't know their gender, race or religion. You could try this in two parts: first, they decide the rules based on being themselves; and then, moving to the 'veil of ignorance', seeing if they would decide the same rules.

---

## Part four: What is fair?

Plato's *Republic* has the question *What is justice?* as a thread running through it, sometimes explicitly and sometimes implicitly, but it is always there. Likewise, the *Republic Island* sessions have the question *What is fair?* running through them. The word 'fair' is a very good replacement word for 'justice' when dealing with children and enables them to engage in similar kinds of discussions without the problem of having to understand the more abstract concept of 'justice'. Sometimes children at the latter end of primary school will introduce the word 'justice' although, and I think it appropriate to use it if they have introduced it themselves although I avoid introducing it otherwise. The word 'fair' is more than adequate for this kind of discussion.

Mention the fact that the word 'fair' has cropped up many times in the 'Island' sessions (if it has). Then say to the children, 'It is about time we stopped to consider what we mean when we say "fair" or "it's not fair!"' Write the word 'fair' in the middle of the board and say: 'So, what is *fair*?' Give the children time to talk to each other about this in groups or pairs. Look out for tensions that arise such as when someone says that 'fair' is when you 'get

Fair?

what you want' and when someone else says that 'fair' is getting 'an equal share' or getting 'what you need'. To help draw out a tension like this ask them a question like: 'If everyone gets equal share would everyone get what they want?' or, conversely: 'If everyone gets what they want would everyone have an equal share?' (See Teaching Strategy *Break the circle* on page 34.)

### Extension Activities

#### Invaders

If you would like to extend these sessions, especially with older children, then introduce some invaders to their island. This could be an aggressive invasion or it could be more of a benign visit. How do the children react to this situation? What do they think they should they do?

#### The invaders' flag

They see the invaders' flag on the boat the invaders arrived in. Tell them how the invaders claim that the island is theirs. Later you could describe one of the survivors finding an old flag somewhere on the island (maybe including evidence of encampment or a settlement), proving that the island had been found by the invaders earlier – before they arrived there. Does this mean that the island really belongs to the invaders? What should they do now?

#### Trade

You could even use this setting for the children to explore trade and its workings. How would they trade with neighbouring islands? What would be a fair way to trade? Would they need currency?

# Online

Main philosophy:
Plato and Justice

Related philosophy:
Aristotle and Friendship
Aristotle and Teleology
Mill and Utilitarianism
Moral Philosophy

 **Related sessions**

The Meaning of Ant Life (page 57)
The Ring of Gyges (page 74)
The Frog and the Scorpion (page 105)

I would like to thank fellow consultants Ruth Oswald for the 'Rawls' rules' extension activity idea and Robert Torrington for the 'Invaders' and 'Trade' Extension Activity ideas.

# The Ring of Gyges

What *would* you do? What *should* you do? What's the difference?

*For Grinling Gibbons Primary School 2007, Lewisham.*

Suitable for age 8 and upwards.
Star rating: **

## Themes

Power
Doing good
Moral responsibility

## Philosophy

Like the previous story, this one is also taken from Plato's *Republic* (Book 2) and is used to great effect to explore a key question in moral philosophy: 'Why should I be good?' Plato pushes this question even further by the use of this story, which is designed to remove the punitive aspect of good behaviour. In other words, how do we respond to the question if we remove the possibility of being caught and punished? It is amazing how much this punitive element creeps into our usual responses to this question. For instance, if somebody suggests we should still be good even if we could get away with not being caught because God is watching us and He knows what we are doing, then they have reintroduced the fear of punishment as a motivating force. Plato wants to know what we should do when this has been completely removed. This highlights a general concern from moral philosophers that doing good is somehow tainted by the motive of avoiding punishment or gaining reward. The question Plato was interested in was: 'Is doing good something that should be pursued for its own sake?' Or, 'Is doing good good in itself?' Socrates thought that it was. The 17th-century Dutch philosopher Spinoza expressed it like this: 'Blessedness is not the reward of virtue: it is virtue itself.' An interesting feature of most superheroes is that they are often anonymous, which means they are greatly motivated by the intrinsic value of doing good rather than for recognition or reward. With this in mind, compare Superman with Batman or Spiderman, or even the Hulk. What are their motives for doing what they do and how do they differ?

---

### Hints and tips: Moralising

When carrying out philosophy sessions, particularly sessions using the concept of morality, it is extremely important to resist the temptation to moralise. This is not to say that there is no place for moralising in teaching, but that it should be avoided during PhiE sessions. It provides a much greater and more effective challenge to children's behaviour and motives to require them to provide reasons for their views on moral behaviour and for them to challenge each other. It is important, however, that they do not feel they might be 'caught out' or condemned for their ideas. If the children detect there might be a particular answer the teacher expects of them, then the session may become unduly influenced by this perceived answer.

---

# Stimulus

*Imagine you are a citizen of Athens, in ancient Greece, called Gyges, and that you like to explore the land around the city. One day you go exploring much further into the wilderness than usual, leaving your home-city of Athens many miles behind you. Eventually you reach an unknown woodland area and decide to look around. After walking in the wood for a few hours you are aware that it is beginning to get dark and, worried that you may get lost in the dark, you start to make your way out of the wood. But it is not long before you realise you are already lost. Eventually, after walking aimlessly for a few more hours, you decide you will have to spend the night in this dark wood before seeking the way out in the morning. You find a cave almost entirely hidden by vines and leaves that leads deep into a cliff-side under a mossy overhang. You light your torch and hold it high before you so that the flames light your way, and you venture into the swallowing darkness of the cave. You walk for about a quarter of a mile, following a winding passage until it eventually opens to reveal a large chamber. Holding your torch in front of you, you notice there are six huge pillars lining either side of the chamber. At the far end is a large throne made of stone that seats a shocking sight: the remains of what must have been an important man, which you can tell by his ornate armour and the huge decorated sword he still clings with his bony hands. He has been there an awfully long time as he is nothing now but a dusty, cobwebbed skeleton grinning at you from under a bronze helmet. Resisting the impulse to run back the way you have come, you step forward to investigate this ancient king, determined to find something as a memento of your incredible adventure. Examining the skeleton you see that on one of its white fingers is a golden ring. You tentatively reach forward and prize the ring from the finger, at which point fear finally grasps you and you turn and run back the way you came. Your footsteps echo in the cave and you are convinced that these echoes are the sound of the skeleton in pursuit. Only when you emerge back into the outside night do you realise it was your imagination playing tricks on you. You settle down to try to get some sleep so you have energy for the journey home in the morning.*

*When you finally return home you make an astonishing discovery: when you put the ring on your finger, you, and all that you wear, become invisible. While you are wearing the ring nobody can see you! You wonder why the skeleton-king was not invisible when you found him, given he was wearing the ring on his finger. You conclude the ring must only work on living things and that the king must have died while invisible. You shudder at the thought.*

The enquiry can be broken into several stages, each one moving closer to the philosophical heart of the issue. The first stage is a bit of fun, but also very revealing.

TQ 1: What would you do with a ring of invisibility?

Write this Task Question in the centre of the board and *concept map* the children's responses. Some classes will offer a variety of responses from 'using it to steal' to 'not taking it because it's not yours'. Others will tend to stay on the theme of mischief and personal gain. Resist the temptation to judge them for this (see the Hints and Tips box, page 75). Follow this with the contrasting second Task Question.

TQ 2: What do you think would be the right thing to do?

Nested Questions:
- Should you do the right thing?
- Should you do just what you want?
- Why is there a difference between the two lists (TQ 1 and TQ 2)?

TQ 3: (Plato's question) If no one knows it's you, should you do whatever you like?
Or if you can't get caught, then would it be okay to do naughty things?

---

### Teaching Strategy: If the fact (page 35)

You will need to use the anchoring technique (see *Anchoring*, page 30. *If the fact*, page 35 and *Removing reintroduced concepts*, page 36) with this question to keep them on track. So, each time somebody inadvertently re-introduces the punitive element (e.g. 'No, you shouldn't, because they might find out later if they find your fingerprints') simply *if the fact*: '*If you knew* that you couldn't be caught, then should you do whatever you like?'

---

TQ 4: Introduce Socrates (469–399 BCE). Explain that he thought you should always do good because it's good to do good and because doing good will make you a happier person. Ask the children what they think of this view and whether they agree or disagree with Socrates about this. Controversially, he thought you should do good even if you suffer greatly for it. What do the children think of that?

Nested Question:
- Should we do good? Why?

# The superhero's question

Read the children the following.

*Imagine you are a superhero. What sort of superhero would you be? What powers would you have? What would your disguise be? What would your costume look like? As a superhero you spend much of your time using your powers to help people in trouble or to save lives helping the police and bringing criminals to justice. One day, you are visited by someone who has exactly the same powers as you. You are amazed, as you thought you were the only person in the world with these powers. You both spend some time explaining to each other how you got your powers before they suggest to you that you do not have to use your powers for the good of others, that you can use your powers to benefit yourself. They say, 'Why waste all that time helping others when your first duty should be to yourself?' Finally, they suggest you team up to become an unstoppable criminal force.*

TQ 5: How would you answer this other superhuman?

## Extension Activities

Set the children the task of inventing their own superhero – including powers and costume – possibly as a drawing exercise.
   Ask the children whether they think they have powers. List them.

TQ 6: How can their powers be used? And, how should their powers be used?
Further TQ: Spiderman's Uncle Ben said: 'With great power comes great responsibility.' What did he mean by this?

# Online

Main philosophy:
Moral Philosophy: Kant and Duty; Bentham and Consequentialism; Aristotle and Virtue Ethics

Related philosophy:
Kant and Moral Luck
Plato and Justice
Sartre, de Beauvoir and Human Nature
Spinoza and Determinism
Socrates, Plato and Weakness of the Will

 **Related Sessions**

Republic Island (page 66)
The Frog and the Scorpion (page 105)
Billy Bash (page 128)
The Ceebie Stories: The Robbery (page 155)
The Ceebie Stories: The Lie (page 166)

# The Prince and the Pig

*For the 2009 Year 2 class at St. Winifred's Infant's School, Lewisham.*

Suitable for ages 5–11.
Star rating: *

## Themes

Happiness
Values
Points of view
Animals

## Philosophy

This story has been written around the following question: 'Is it better to be a human dissatisfied or a satisfied pig?' This theme has been derived from a discussion the philosopher John Stuart Mill (1806–1873) includes in his book *Utilitarianism*. The story asks us to consider how important happiness is in our lives. If happiness is all that matters, then maybe we should choose to be the happy pig. However, we may have reservations about this because we may find we lose something more important such as our dignity or our ability to make choices. Alternatively, we may think that no matter how happy we are as a pig the possibility of becoming a sausage on someone's plate is a price too high to pay, but then you may think that if you are dead, then that would not matter. This gives you an idea of some of the directions in which this discussion can go (and has done in sessions I have run).

Mill's own answer was that it is always better to be the dissatisfied human because, for him, the quality of the pleasure is more important than the quantity of it, and humans are better equipped to experience higher quality pleasures. Even if the pig were to have more pleasure more of the time, that would not make up for the quality of the pleasure that a human is capable of having, even if the human were not happy all of the time. Mill also believed that someone who has experienced both sides of the argument – in other words, someone who had been both a happy pig and an unhappy human – would always choose to be the human over the pig. He thought this could be argued for purely on the grounds of considering the nature of the kinds of experience they would be – that is to say, he did not think you needed to actually become a pig and then a human to answer it; all you have to do is consider it. This is an important part of the practice of philosophy: it tries to see what can be done and what answers can be achieved just by thought alone. If, unlike Mill, you conclude this could only be resolved by being able to experience being a pig, then that would mean you think this is not a philosophical question.

# Stimulus

*Long ago, there was once a prince called Nikolai, who was forever miserable. He was always grumpy and unpleasant to everyone around him and was always feeling sad. Even though he had many beautiful things, he felt that everyone else had more reason than him to be happy no matter how rich or poor they were. Every night he would cry himself to sleep and dream dreams that brought a frown to his sleeping face.*

*One day his father, the king, told him at supper that he must take being a prince much more seriously. 'One day you will rule these lands,' he said sternly, 'and so you must learn to rule as a king. You must stop all this moping around or I will make your sister queen instead. One day you must marry the princess of the kingdom of Algia to secure an alliance with Algia, and later you will have to lead our armies to the border of our kingdom to protect it from the barbarians. You may not want to do these things but it will be your duty to do them as king.'*

*Grumpy and upset, Prince Nikolai went off to the court barnyard where he knew he would be left alone. He sat on a hay bale and watched the animals, all of which he thought were happier than him, and he tried to decide which was the happiest of all the barnyard animals. The hens were always pecking each other because they wanted to be at the top of the pecking order. The dogs were always barking at people and animals that got too close to them tied up in their kennels. The pigs, however, seemed the most content squelching in the mud looking for grubs, roots and truffles with their large snouts. Feeling very sorry for himself, Nikolai said, spitefully, 'I wish I was a happy pig!'*

*It just so happened that at that very moment there was a passing genie, unseen to any human eye, travelling invisibly through the air on a cloud. The genie heard the wish as the prince uttered it, and if you know anything about genies you will know they are bound by an ancient law to answer the wishes of any wish-maker they happen to hear.*

*Suddenly, the genie appeared in front of the prince. Nikolai froze in astonishment as the magical servant materialised before his eyes. 'So, you want to be a happy pig instead of an unhappy boy. Well, I can make your wish come true,' said the genie cheerfully as he lifted his finger as if to cast a spell.*

*'But ... but ... no. Wait!' stammered the prince, now not quite so sure whether he wanted his wish to come true.*

*The genie stopped and said: 'I am sorry, but now that you have made the wish I have to make it come true, because I heard you say it. Those are the rules.'*

*'But I don't want to become a dirty pig, happy or not!' protested the prince.*

*'Here's what I can do,' said the genie, trying to be helpful. 'I can give you a condition: I will not change you into a pig if, by the time I return tomorrow, you can think of one good reason why it is better to be an unhappy person rather than a happy pig. If you cannot think of a good reason, then a pig you shall become. But remember, you'll be very happy and will have all that you could wish for until the day you die. You have until tomorrow at sunset to think about it.' With that the genie vanished as mysteriously as he had appeared.*

*Nikolai thought about what the genie had said. And he thought, and then he thought some more. The following question hovered over him all night and all of the next day: 'Is it better to be an unhappy person or a happy pig?' At first it seemed like a simple question which was easy to answer. But the more he thought about it, the more difficult it was for him to answer.*

At this point, the story should be stopped so the children can consider the question for themselves (as if they were in Prince Nikolai's situation). Encourage them to come up with as many 'for' and 'against' reasons as they can.

> TQ 1: Is it better to be an unhappy person or a happy pig?

This should form the bulk of the session, but reserve 5 minutes or so at the end to tell the rest of the story.

> ### Teaching Strategy: Imaginary disagreer (page 32)
>
> If you find the class reaches unanimity on this question – for instance, if they all think it would be better to be a human – then try the *imaginary disagreer* strategy, but with the entire class. Ask them what reasons someone might give if they thought it better to be a happy pig. This will encourage them to consider other points of view at the same time as keeping the discussion moving and more interesting. (See also Teaching Strategy *Sympathise and criticise*, page 45 for a useful way around unanimity.)

*The next evening, as promised, the genie reappeared. 'Have you thought of one good reason why it is better to be an unhappy boy rather than a happy pig?' demanded the genie. Desperately, Nikolai searched his mind one last time for a good reason, but he could not think of one. The genie announced dutifully: 'Then I must, as bound by the ancient law of magic, make your wish come true.' He waved his finger as he had begun to the day before and continued: 'Come tomorrow, you will awake in the barnyard happier than you have ever been.' Even though he would be happy, Nikolai was still scared of the idea of becoming a pig with hooves, a snout and a curly tail condemned forever to have his face stuck in the dirt.*

*'ALLAKAZOOM!' said the genie and then he was gone.*

Read the following slowly to build the suspense and allow the children's apprehension to grow.

*Morning comes and the first sound he hears is the cockerel crowing heralding the start of the new day. He opens his eyes slowly and sees animals all around him. He is indeed in the barnyard, just as the genie had said. He lifts up what he thinks will be a hoof ... but sees only a boy's hand. He runs to the well and peers into the water to see his new snouty reflection ... but is surprised to see only his princely face. It seems the genie had tricked him. The prince jumps up immediately and dances around the farmyard singing joyfully at the top of his voice, hugging and kissing the animals with relief.*

*Then he starts to notice that he is experiencing a completely new feeling; one that he has never felt before. He looks back down the well and asks his reflection: 'Is this happiness?'*

TQ or SQ: Has Nikolai found happiness?

Has Nikolai found happiness?

Nested Questions:
- What is happiness?
- Will it last?
- How can you make happiness last?

### Teaching Strategy: Identify and challenge assumptions (page 36)

The Task Question for this story is actually incorporated into the story itself. The story is a thought experiment designed to invite the children to consider the value of happiness in their lives and, by implication, other surrounding values. The sort of assumption that one may expect to find emerging from this discussion is: *happiness follows from doing what you want*. You may expect something like the following line of reasoning.

A (Child): He should stay a prince because one day he will be king.
B (Facilitator): Why is being a king important?
A: Because when he is king he can do whatever he wants and then he'll be happy.
B: Do you think doing whatever you want will make you happy?
A: Yes.
B: Why?
A: Because then he can tell people what to do and get them to do things for him.

In this discussion the assumption that 'you will be happy when you can do what you want' has been made explicit and would itself make an excellent Task Question: 'Would you be happy if you could do exactly what you wanted?' But there is a further assumption here that has remained implicit: for this particular speaker *controlling others is necessary for happiness*. So, if the child is persuaded at a later stage that it's better to be a happy pig on the condition the pig gets exactly what it wants at all times, it may turn out that the child would still not want to be a pig because the pig could not tell anyone what to do.

Once an assumption such as *you will be happy if you can do what you want* has been identified, then turning it into a Task Question helps to move the discussion to the next stage: *challenging the assumption*. Having the assumption put before them in this way will instantly invite the children to seek alternatives to it such as: 'If you do what you want it might not be what other people want, and if everyone does what they want it might not be what you want, so "doing what you want" doesn't always make you happy' (10 year-old girl).

# Online

Main philosophy:
Mill and Utilitarianism

Related philosophy:
Aristotle and Teleology
Aristotle and Virtue Ethics
Bentham and Consequentialism
Sartre, de Beauvoir and Human Nature

 **Related sessions**

The Ring of Gyges (page 74)
Goldfinger (page 98)
The Frog and the Scorpion (page 105)
The Happy Prisoner (page 93)
The Meaning of Ant Life (page 57)

# The Ship of Theseus

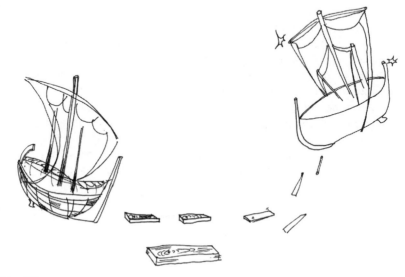

Ship of Theseus

*For the 2009 Year 5 class at Horniman Primary School, Lewisham.*

Suitable for age 9 and upwards.
Star rating: **

## Themes

Identity
Personal identity
Change

## Philosophy

The Ship of Theseus was famously supplied as a philosophical thought experiment by the British philosopher Thomas Hobbes. He drew the example from

Plutarch, a Roman writer. Theseus comes from Greek mythology and is the same Theseus who defeated the Minotaur with the help of Ariadne.

In order for this session to be philosophically fruitful it is necessary to understand the philosophical subtleties involved in an exploration of the thought experiment. Read the stimulus below before reading on. The Nested Question to bear in mind in this enquiry is: 'If it is a new ship when all the parts are replaced, then at what point does it become a new ship?'

This is where a lot of the philosophy will lie because here we are faced with the 'problem of vagueness'. If it is a new ship when the parts are all replaced and only then, would that mean that when it only had one part left to replace, it was still the old ship? If so, this seems a little odd. If not, then when does it become the new ship? This particular problem is a version of what is known as the *sorites paradox* (from the Greek word for 'heap'): 'How many grains of sand make a heap?'

---

 **Teaching Strategy: If the idea – 'Let's test it' (page 35)**

For the purpose of keeping things clear for the discussion, it is a good idea to illustrate all this with examples as you go. I would ask the children to imagine the ship has 100 parts (for the sake of argument). You can then use this at each point of the discussion to have them explore and reach the difficulties for themselves. For example, if someone says it would be the new ship when more than half the parts are replaced, *if the idea* to test it: 'Let's test it: if it has 51 new parts and only 49 old parts then is it a new ship?' Ask the class what they think about this.

---

This session is subtly changed if, during your presentation of the stimulus, you say the ship is replaced simply with new parts of the same material, so: wood for wood. The emphasis is on *identity* in this case, whereas the emphasis is on *vagueness* when the replaced parts are metal. I usually stick to the 'metal' version of the story for primary school children, as it is easier for them to conceptualise the problem. It becomes difficult to refer to the two ships if they are both made of the same stuff. You could try it both ways by altering the stimulus accordingly.

# Stimulus

*Theseus owned a ship and the ship was entirely made of wood. He sailed around the ocean for many years in his ship. Every time a piece of the ship needed replacing it was replaced with a metal part. This went on for a few years until eventually it was entirely replaced.*

> TQ 1: Is the ship of Theseus the same ship of Theseus as it was when it was first built?

It may be helpful to draw a diagram similar to the one below as you explain the scenario and write the Task Question underneath.

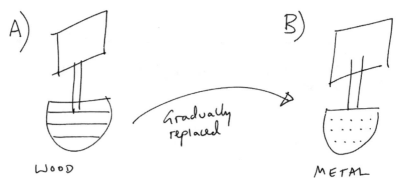

Is the ship of Theseus the same ship of Theseus as when it was first built?

There are very likely to be some *materialists* aboard your classroom – that is to say, those who will maintain that the ship is different if it is made of different stuff: 'It was made of wood but now it's made of metal.' Thomas Hobbes was also a materialist in his response to the problem. He proposed a version of the following thought experiment to anyone who would entertain that the metal ship is the same as the wooden ship.

*On board the ship was a sailor who really wanted his own ship but could not afford one. So, he came up with a plan: every time Theseus decided to replace one of the wooden parts of his ship with a metal part, the sailor would take the discarded piece of wood and hide it in his shed. When eventually he had collected all the wooden parts he re-assembled them into a ship again.*

> TQ 2: Does this mean there are two ships of Theseus or one? Which is the ship of Theseus?

Again, use diagrams to explain all this:

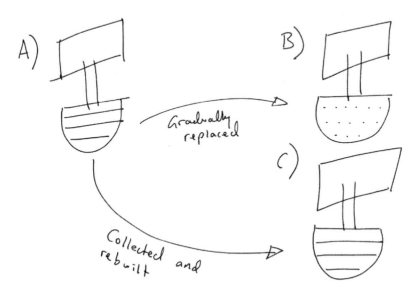

A)

B)

C)

Gradually replaced

Collected rebuilt and

Which one is the ship of Theseus?

The sorts of ideas you might expect to hear in this session are as follows (often in different words).

- The ship is different the moment the first plank is replaced because any change would result in a different ship. Later, when you move to a discussion of personhood, a **Response Question** (RQ) to this point could be: 'Does that mean that any change to myself/yourself, such as a tooth falling out, makes me/you a different person?'
- The ship is different only when the last piece has been replaced because only then none of the original ship is left. RQ: 'Does that mean that when there is only one piece of the original ship left it is still the old ship?'
- If the ship *suddenly* changed into metal then it would be different, but if it changes *gradually* then it is the same ship because, at each stage of change, it is related to the old ship in that it is only minutely different.
- Even though the material it is made of changes, the shape, the name and the design stay the same, so it is the same ship.
- It is the same ship if people *think* it's the same ship.

# The 'Self' of Theseus

At some point you will want to talk about how the discussion of the ship pertains to how we think of ourselves. This will either happen very naturally when the children start to make the connection or you will need to make the connection explicit yourself. Here are some suggestions of how it can be done.

- Show two photographs next to each other of someone as a young child and as an old person. Ask the children whether they think this is the same person and why.
- If you are with older children (age 10 upwards), you can explain how scientists tell us that our cells (explain what these are) are completely replaced every seven years or so and then ask the children if this means they are a different person every seven years.

   The key Nested Question here is:
   What is it that makes us the same person at different times?

Possible responses to this problem are as follows.

- *People* and *things* are different.

RQ: How are they different?

- People have thoughts and memories but ships don't.
- We might change on the outside but our personalities stay the same.

RQ: Does this mean our personalities can't change?

A suggested Task Question to deepen this enquiry follows.

TQ 3: Where is the 'me bit' inside of us?

One 11 year-old girl said in answer to this: 'The "me bit" is the thoughts inside my head.' (See companion website: Descartes and Dualism, 'I think therefore I am.')

Each of these insights can lead to further related discussions in themselves.

The philosopher John Locke (1632–1704) believed that we are linked by memory to our past selves, which makes us the same person through time. So, for Locke, it is not our body that makes us the same person – as this is constantly changing – but our mental life that lasts through change. RQ: 'If we lose our memory would that make us a different person?'

---

 ### Hints and Tips: Concrete and personalised discussions

Children may begin to lose interest if philosophy discussions are too abstract or seem irrelevant to their own experience. So it is often good to begin with concrete examples, such as – in this session – a scenario with a repaired ship where the philosophical problems always have a concrete reference for the children to test them out. Also, making the discussions about the children in some way can keep them engaged with the issues. Putting the insights and ideas about the ship into the context of their own lives and experience can bring it vividly to life for them. Many of the children will have been thinking along these lines already and it can be reassuring for those children to find that there is a whole tradition of thinking about these ideas stretching back many hundreds – in some cases, thousands – of years.

It is important, however, to make sure you never personalise the discussions. If a child introduces an example around another child, it is often better to gently ask them to make the example about someone fictitious.

---

# Online

Main philosophy:
Hobbes and Materialism

Related philosophy:
Berkley and Idealism
Descartes and Dualism
Heraclitus and Change
Leibniz and Identity
Socrates, Aristotle and the Soul
Zeno, Paradoxes and Infinity

**Related sessions**

# The Happy Prisoner

A prison with everything you could want

*For the 2008 Year 5 class at John Ball Primary School, Lewisham.*

Suitable for age 9 and upwards.
Star rating: **

## Themes

Freedom
Freedom of the will
Moral responsibility

## Philosophy

This is an adaptation of a thought experiment (by John Locke) known as
'the voluntary prisoner'. It is designed to draw an important distinction

between voluntary action and free will. It is often supposed that voluntary action shows we have free will but Locke's example challenges this intuition. The prisoner is in the prison voluntarily but not freely. In other words, he chooses to stay there but would not be able to leave if he chose to do so. This identifies a key idea in the philosophy of free will: the concept of 'could have done otherwise'. For many philosophers it is not the fact that we make choices that is required to prove we have a free will, but whether or not we could have done other than we did in fact do. This is complex stuff and the philosophical view that we have no free will is known as *determinism*.

The aim of this session is not to make the children understand the complex and intractable problem of determinism but for them to explore the concept of freedom for themselves and hopefully to identify, in their own ways, different notions of freedom.

## Stimulus

*Imagine a man who is taken, in his sleep, to a prison. When he awakes he finds that the prison has everything he would want: books, television, kitchen, a comfortable bed, and an endless supply of his favourite music (to name just a few of the things he has). He even finds he is sharing a cell with another prisoner who he likes very much and who likes him; they both enjoy the same things and really like talking to each other. However, if the man were to try to leave the prison he would be unable to. But he does not want to leave; he is very happy there. So, we have a man in a prison who is very happy to be there and has no desire to leave, but, if he did want to, he would be unable to.*

> TQ 1: Is the man free?

I have heard the following starting responses when teaching this session.

- The man is not free because he cannot do what he wants.

> RQ: Are you only free when you can do what you want?

- He is free in his mind but not physically.
- He is not free because if he got bored with the things he has in the prison he can't go and do something else.

RQ: If he never got bored with the things he has in the prison and was happy there his whole life, would that mean he was free or not? (See the Teaching Strategy box at the end of this session: *If the idea*.)

- He is not free because he cannot see his family.
- He is not free because his family cannot see him. (Notice the subtle difference between these two ideas: in the former formulation he is not free because of what he wants but in the latter formulation he is not free because of what other people he is related to might want of him.)
- *In a way* he is free and *in a way* he is not free. Here are some reasons given for this view:
  - Free because he is happy and not free because he can't leave the prison.
  - Free because he can go where he wants in the prison but not free because he can't go out of it.
  - Free because he has rights and not free because he is trapped in the prison.
  - He is not free because he's a prisoner and 'prisoner' means 'not free'.

---

### Hints and tips: Drawing distinctions

Children often say (or words to this effect): 'In a way *yes* and in a way *no*.' This may at first seem contradictory. However, this is a good sign that they have begun to dissolve the apparent dichotomy in the discussion (see *Dissolving dichotomies*, page 38), and is usually an indication that they are drawing distinctions, or at least drawing attention to the fact that distinctions need to be drawn. In this example they are intimating that there is more than one meaning of 'free' present in the discussion, or they are introducing more than one meaning of 'free' for their own purposes. Always ask clarification questions (e.g. 'Can you explain what you mean by . . . ?') when you suspect a distinction beginning to be drawn.

---

TQ 2: Are *we* free?
(This question can be used for this, or a follow-up, session.)

Expect the children to identify rules and restrictions on our behaviour and conduct as a reason why we are not free. However, as one Year 6 pupil pointed out: 'There are rules, but some people break them. So, we are free.' An important distinction to be aware of in this discussion is that between the *ability to do something* and *moral freedom*. It is not possible for us to fly like a bird but it is possible to steal from shops, even though it is against the law. It may be morally wrong to steal and there may be consequences for stealing but it is not beyond our power to steal.

---

### Teaching Strategy: If the idea (page 35)

The thinking strategy *if the fact* described in the Teaching Strategies section (page 29) is an invaluable technique for avoiding the problem of the facts in a discussion. However, there is another subtler use of this strategy – not to do with facts but to do with ideas. This session provides an example of *if the idea* to deepen thinking. A child says that the prisoner is not free because he can't go out of the prison if he wants to – for instance, if he gets bored with what he has in the prison. To encourage further thinking on this you could say, 'Let's think about this. *If* he went through his whole life and was happy in the prison and never wanted to leave, *then* would he have been free or not?' In this particular instance one child was then galvanised to further thought that led to the following insight: 'No, because he didn't have the option or opportunity to do something.' The child had identified the crucial feature of *option* or *opportunity* as essential for freedom, which, as you may notice, resembles Locke's own position on this: that free will is not just what we *choose* to do but what we are *able* to do, what options are, in fac,t open to us.

You can also use the *iffing* strategy for questions the children may ask about the scenario. Imagine a child asks: 'Does the prisoner know he is in a prison?' You may at first feel as though you should answer the question, but it is best to simply turn this into a thinking exercise for the questioner: '*If* the prisoner doesn't know he is a prisoner, then would that mean that he is free or not?' The key is not to worry about what the facts are but to get the children thinking about what a supposed fact would mean for any issue under consideration. *Iffing* is an extremely useful way of achieving this in the classroom.

---

# Online

Main philosophy:
Locke and Free Will

Related philosophy:
Hobbes and Materialism
Sartre, de Beauvoir and Human Nature (on choice)

Socrates, Plato and Weakness of the Will
Spinoza and Determinism

---

 **Related sessions**

The Prince and the Pig (page 80)
The Frog and the Scorpion (page 105)
The Little Old Shop of Curiosities (page 111)
Billy Bash (page 128)
The Ceebie Stories: The Robbery (page 155)

# Goldfinger

*For the 2009 Year 2 class at Ashmead Primary School, Lewisham.*

Suitable for ages 5–9.
Star rating: *

## Themes

Language
Meaning
Precision and accuracy
Happiness
Wishes

## Philosophy

There are many branches of philosophy and schools of thought – from rationalism and empiricism to existentialism and postmodernism. One of the most influential movements to emerge in the 20th century has become known as *analytic philosophy*, which concerns itself with the logical analysis of sentence structure and meaning, along with the concepts that determine them. Many analytic philosophers believe that philosophical problems boil down to the meaning of sentences and our relationship to them. This session is inspired by the philosophical demand for greater accuracy and precision of language. The objectives behind this session are to encourage young children to formulate critical responses to each other so they can see the importance of accurate language and begin to improve the precision of the structure and content of their sentences.

## Stimulus

*This is the story of a king, many years ago in ancient Greece, whose name was Midas. Midas was the ruler of a huge kingdom that stretched for miles around,*

King Midas

*and one thing you need to know about King Midas was that he loved gold more than almost anything else in the world. He collected enough gold to fill the vaults below his palace and he would often hide away in these vaults to count his gold over and over again.*

*Around his palace Midas had a large beautiful garden filled with pretty flowers, trees and statues. One day a centaur (a mythical creature with the upper body of a man and the lower body of a horse) wandered into a hidden corner of Midas's garden, lay down in the soft grass and fell asleep. The gardeners noticed the creature sleeping on the grass and they thought of a nasty plan to make fun of him. They crept up on him and tied up his ankles and wrists. Then they took a long stick and violently poked him, pointing and laughing while the centaur wriggled and writhed on the ground.*

*It so happened that, at that time, King Midas was walking through his garden admiring the beautiful flowers when he noticed some commotion in the far corner. He marched forward to see what was happening. When he saw what his gardeners were doing to the stranger he was furious: 'STOP THAT AT ONCE!' He shouted. 'I will not have that sort of thing happening in my kingdom! Untie him immediately!'*

The gardeners quaked in their boots, afraid of their king and what he might do to punish them. They quickly obeyed his command and untied the helpless stranger.

The centaur fell to his knees before Midas and said: 'Thank you, your highness, for saving me from that humiliation. I am Silenus, servant to the God Dionysus, who lives on Mount Olympus with all the other gods. When he finds out what you have done for me, I am sure he will be very pleased with you.'

When Silenus returned to his master and explained what had happened, Dionysus said, in a booming, god-like voice, 'This Midas is indeed a good man and to show my gratitude for saving my servant I want you, Silenus, to return to him and grant him one single wish. It can be anything his heart desires but it must only be one single wish. Now go!' Silenus went back down the mountain and returned to Midas's palace.

'Midas,' he said. 'My master is pleased with you and would like to grant you any one single wish you may desire. But you only get one wish.'

It did not take Midas long to think of a wish. He said, quickly and without thinking, 'I wish that everything I touch will turn to gold.'

'It is done,' said Silenus and with that he left to return to his master.

Of course, Midas did not believe his wish had come true, so he reached over and touched the nearest thing to him, which was a statue. Ding! It turned to gold right before his eyes. Astonished, King Midas said out loud, 'I will be the richest man in all of Greece.' Then he thought about it and said, 'No, I will be the richest man in all the world!'

Midas set about touching everything he could see in his garden. He touched tables: 'Ding!' Statues: 'Ding!' Bushes: 'Ding!' And trees: 'Ding!' Everything he could think of" 'Ding! Ding! Ding-d-ding-ding-ding!' He was dinging things for maybe two or three hours until eventually he stopped – his garden glistening with gold – and said, rubbing his tummy, 'All this turning-things-into-gold is hungry, thirsty work. I think I will stop for a rest.' He ordered his servants to bring a feast of breads, meats, wines and fruits and to place them on his new golden table. He had the wine poured into his new golden goblet and he sat down on his new golden chair, lifted a goblet to his lips and drank. Ding! As the wine touched his lips it turned to gold. 'I can't drink this!' he exclaimed, and he reached for a grape. But as he plucked it from the bunch: Ding! It also turned to gold. 'I can't eat this!' He said, staring in horror at the golden grape. Slowly, he realised what he had done. 'Oh no,' he moaned, 'I can never eat or drink again. What have I done? What have I done?' He put his head in his hands and slumped down on his table moaning about what had befallen him.

*Now, there was only one thing in the whole world that Midas loved more than gold, and that was his beautiful daughter. As he was moaning about his terrible fate, his daughter came along and saw him, slumped on the table. She did not like to see her father upset, so, she thought to herself, 'I know, what my father needs is a big hug and a kiss. That will cheer him up.' She crept up to him and just before she reached him she stepped on a twig – click. He looked up, but before he could say anything she had hugged him. Ding! Before his very eyes his beautiful daughter stood there frozen – a solid, golden kissing statue. Midas fell to his knees and sobbed. 'Now all the joy in the world for me is gone,' he said. 'What have I done? What have I done?'*

At this point say something like the following: 'I am going to stop the story here, but don't worry, you will find out what happens to King Midas later. Right now, I'd like us to think about the story and then talk about it, so we can share our ideas. So, what went wrong for Midas?'

Spend a few minutes letting the children explain what they think went wrong and allow them to explore their own understanding of the story. So, if

Frozen in a golden kiss

someone asks a question about the story, ask the other children to answer it. After a few minutes set them the following task.

'In the story Midas makes a wish; he wished that everything he touched would turn to gold.' Write up on the board his precise wish.

King Midas: 'I wish that everything I touch will turn to gold.'

Underneath this write:

'I wish ...'

Now say to the children: 'I want you to imagine you are King Midas. Can you think of another way that you could say the wish so that it would not go so wrong?' Alternatively, say 'Is there another way you could say the wish so that it would not go wrong?' Say this while pointing to your 'I wish ...' on the board.

Ask the children to discuss this for a few minutes in pairs or groups before sharing and take the time to find out what they think. Encourage them, in their pairs, to seek problems with wishes. So, whenever someone suggests a version of the wish ('I wish that everything I touch will turn to gold except for my food and my drink') encourage the others to examine whether the wish could still go wrong: 'Is there any way that this wish could still go wrong?' ('Yes, his daughter would still turn to gold.')

When you return to a full-class discussion, continue by finding out new formulations of the wish and asking others if it could still go wrong. Try to detect responses to this question before finding out what their wish would be. One aim of this session is to encourage very young children to formulate a response to other children. Here are some examples of the sorts of wishes you may expect to hear from ages 5 and 6.

- 'I wish that everything I touch would turn to gold except for my food and my drink and my daughter.'
- 'I wish that everything I touch would turn to gold except for things that I need.'
- 'I wish that everything I touch would turn to gold but when I touch it again it will turn back again.'
- 'I wish that only things I want to turn to gold will turn to gold when I touch them.'

---

### Teaching Strategy: Concept play (page 37)

One suggestion from a 5-year old child was: 'Midas should wish for only *objects* to turn to gold.' Here, you could engage them with some *conceptual analysis*. The question to ask in order to do this would be:

'What is an object?' Another way of doing this is to play *Break the circle* (page 34) on the word 'object'. Alternatively, here are some suggested questions for engaging the children in some concept-play.

- If Midas wished for only objects to turn to gold, what sort of things would turn to gold and what sort of things wouldn't?
- [Pupil's name] said that Midas should have wished for only objects to turn to gold. What would happen to his daughter then? Is she an object?
- 'Is a grape an object? What about water?'
- 'Are we objects?'

Remember always to follow questions like these with elicitation questions such as 'Why?' and 'Can you explain why?' or 'What do you mean by . . .' etc. (See *Opening up closed questions*, page 41.)

Leave yourself 5 minutes before the end of the session to finish the story.

*So, Midas was on his knees sobbing. In fact, he stayed like that for three whole days, he was so upset.*

*Meanwhile, the god Dionysus – who, if you remember, granted Midas's wish in the first place – had been watching this sorry tale unfold from on top of Mount Olympus. Eventually, he turned to his servant and said, 'Silenus, I want you to return to Midas and tell him that I have taken pity on him. After all, the wish was supposed to be a reward for doing a good thing. Tell him I shall reverse the wish.'*

*Silenus went back down the mountain and found Midas still on his knees sobbing.*

*'Midas,' he said, 'my master has taken pity on you and will reverse the wish, but you must go and touch all the things you have already turned to gold to turn them back again.'*

*'Tell your master, "Thank you!"' Midas said, and with that he leapt to his feet straight away, and the first thing he touched was his daughter. He kissed her many times before he set to work touching all the golden items in his garden and palace. And instead of going 'Ding!' each time he touched something, this time, it went 'Fud!'*

*It took Midas much longer to turn everything back than it did to turn every-thing into gold, but when he finally finished he did not even ask for another wish, he was just grateful that everything was back to normal and that his daughter had been returned to him. And, as you may have guessed, Midas did not much like gold anymore. So he decided to take all the gold that he had hoarded over the years and give it to all the poor people in his kingdom.*

Nested Questions:
- Would you be happy if you got what you wanted?
- If you were offered a wish, would you dare to make one or would you be too scared?
- If someone said, 'I wish that everything I touch will turn to gold but if I don't want it to be gold anymore I can make it go back', would it be one single wish or would it be two wishes?
- What is a wish?
- Can we make wishes come true?

## Online

Main philosophy:
Frege, Russell and Logic

Related philosophy:
Aristotle and the Logical Syllogism
Mill and Utilitarianism

 **Related Sessions**

The Meaning of Ant Life (page 57)
The Prince and the Pig (page 80)
The Shadow of the Pyramid (page 117)

# The Frog and the Scorpion

The frog kept a safe distance

*For the 2007 Year 6 class at Sandhurst Primary School, Lewisham.*

Suitable for any age group.
Star rating: *

## Themes

Nature/nurture
Free will
Choice
Moral responsibility
Self-interest
Self-control
Weakness of the will

# Philosophy

This is a traditional story with a great deal of rich thinking material packed into it. Its origins are unclear though it is thought by some to be one of Aesop's fables. What is great about this story is that it is emotionally engaging in that both of the characters come to a sticky end and the story remains ambiguous about how it should be read. But, despite all this, it seems to be very philosophically focused. The central idea that emerges from this story (although there are many other ideas) relates to the impact of our nature on the conception of the moral responsibility that we have. It might seem that if we have a fixed character that issues from forces and motives deep within us, then maybe we shouldn't be held morally responsible for our actions and, conversely, if we are free to choose exactly what we do aren't we therefore fully responsible for what we do? Or is there some other way of understanding our choices and responsibility? Do not try to get the children to understand this. Rather, allow them to explore the issues in their own way.

# Stimulus

*One day a scorpion needed to get across a river to reach her family, but scorpions can't swim. The scorpion saw a frog swimming in the river and asked if he would help the scorpion across. The frog said, 'Gribbit. You're a scorpion and scorpions sting frogs. Gribbit.'*

*To which the scorpion replied, 'But I need your help, so I won't sting you today.'*

*'But how do I know – gribbit – that you won't sting me when you are on my back,' inquired the frog.*

*'Because then you will drown and if I am on your back then so will I,' reasoned the scorpion.*

*'But how do I know – gribbit – that you won't wait until we're on the other side and then sting me?' asked the frog.*

*'Because by then I will be grateful and I'll "owe you one",' assured the scorpion.*

*'How do I know – gribbit – that you won't just sting me anyway?' asked the frog.*

*'You have my word,' said the scorpion finally.*

*The frog thought about it for a while and then said, 'That's good enough for me. Hop on.'*

*The frog swam to the bank and turned around lifting his back towards the scorpion. The scorpion climbed on and the frog began to swim across the river.*

*When they reached roughly half way the frog felt a sudden sharp pain in his side. He realised he had been stung by the scorpion and managed to say with his last breaths: 'What did you do that for? Now we're both going to drown!'*

*The scorpion replied, 'I'm sorry, I couldn't help it – it's in my nature.' And with that both the scorpion and the frog sank to a watery end.*

TQ 1: Who do you think was to blame for the frog and the scorpion's deaths?

Nested Questions:
• What is blame?
• When is something somebody's fault?
• Is 'fault' the same as 'responsibility'?
• If you can't help doing something, is it your fault if you do it?

Some will blame the frog for letting the scorpion on his back – they think he should have known better. Some will blame the scorpion for breaking her word. Some don't blame anyone because the frog was persuaded and the scorpion was acting on instinct. One insight I heard was that the scorpion did not break her word because when she made the promise she meant it and tried very hard to override her instincts. The point is, she *failed* to do so, not that she broke her word. (See companion website: Socrates, Plato and Weakness of the Will.)

# The Robber and the Ferryman

Suitable for age 7 and upwards.

This adaptation of the scorpion and frog story is designed to get the children thinking about the difference between animals and humans from a moral point of view.

*One day a robber needed to get across a dangerous river to escape an angry farmer he had robbed, but the robber couldn't swim. The robber saw a ferryman waiting for customers at the side of the river and asked the ferryman if he would help him across. The ferryman recognised the man as a 'wanted' robber. He saw that the robber had a knife and said, 'You're a robber and robbers rob people.'*

*To which the robber replied, 'But I need your help, so I won't rob you today.'*

'But how do I know you won't wait until we're on the other side and then rob me?' asked the ferryman.

'Because by then I will be grateful and I'll "owe you one",' assured the robber.

'How do I know you won't just rob me anyway?' asked the suspecting ferryman.

'You have my word,' said the robber finally.

The ferryman thought about it for a while and then said, 'That's good enough for me. Get in.'

So the robber climbed into the boat and the ferryman began to row across the river. When they had reached about half way, the ferryman felt a sudden sharp pain in his side. He realised he had been stabbed by the robber, who now had the ferryman's money-bag. With his last breaths the ferryman managed to say, 'Why did you do that? Now we're both done for! The river will surely claim us both.'

The robber replied, 'I couldn't help it – it's in my nature.' And with that both the robber and the ferryman were swept away by the raging current of the river and never seen again.

TQ 2: Who is to blame for the ferryman and robber's deaths in this story?

Nested Questions:
- Is your answer different from the answer given in the first story (about the scorpion and the frog)? Why?
- Does the fact that the characters are now human change anything about who is to blame?

Further thoughts for enquiry:

- If your friend hits you, is it your friend's fault that you get hurt?
- If your cat scratches you, is it the cat's fault that you get scratched?
- If a chair breaks when you sit on it, is it the chair's fault that you fall off?

# The Friend and the Thief

Suitable for age 9 upwards.

This story contrasts well with *the frog and scorpion* version. It touches on social issues as well as those mentioned earlier.

*There were once two friends who had known each other since childhood. As they grew up their paths diverged and one of them, Ben, became educated and went to university while the other, Jeff, pursued a life of crime. Jeff was caught committing a serious burglary and went to prison for a number of years. When he eventually left prison he called up his only friend, Ben, and said he wanted to get his life back on track. Jeff vowed he would leave his life of crime behind him. Ben said that if Jeff really meant to keep his promise, then he would help him out. He gave him enough money to last for four months and offered him a room in his house for free – just until Jeff got himself a job and was able to look after himself. Ben kept a secret stash of savings in his house and one day when he returned from work he found this cash had gone, along with Jeff. All that was left was a note on the table. It read: 'I am sorry to have let you down, but I couldn't help it – it's in my nature. One day I'll pay you back.' (Signed) Jeff.*

TQ 3: Could Jeff have stopped himself from taking Ben's savings?

Nested Question:
• Are humans different from scorpions morally speaking?

When I have read and discussed these stories, I introduce children to three philosophers and three accompanying central ideas to focus their thinking.

---

### Philosophy: Human nature

1 Schopenhauer: 'fixed character' – we just do what we do because of what we are like, what kind of person we are. We cannot change our character.
2 Sartre: 'individual choice' – we are free to choose what we do and also what sort of person we become.
3 Aristotle: 'learned habits' – we learn or get certain habits from our parents and friends so if we want to change a habit, we can, but it's not easy.

Some agree with Schopenhauer that 'it's in his head somewhere', as one child once said, but most see it as a mixture, if not of all three then certainly of 2 and 3 ('choice' and 'habit'). They often recognize that choice is important but that choices are not necessarily easy because of one's background.

## Online

Main philosophy:
Locke and Free Will

Related philosophy:
Aristotle and Teleology
Kant and Moral luck
Moral Philosophy
Sartre, de Beauvoir and Human Nature
Socrates, Plato and Weakness of the Will
Spinoza and Determinism

---

 **Related sessions**

The Meaning of Ant Life (page 57)
The Ring of Gyges (page 74)
The Happy Prisoner (page 93)
The Little Old Shop of Curiosities (page 111)
Billy Bash (page 128)
The Ceebie Stories: The Robbery (page 155)
The Ceebie Stories: The Lie (page 166)

# The Little Old Shop of Curiosities

You were sure it wasn't there before

*For the 2010 Year 6 class at St. Winifred's Junior School, Lewisham.*

Suitable for age 10 and upwards.
Star rating: **

## Themes:

The future
The self
Choice
Free will

# The philosophy

This story is adapted from a thought experiment by Alvin Goldman called 'The Book of Life'. He uses this experiment to explore the nature of human freedom in the context of a philosophical doctrine known as *determinism*. This doctrine holds that there is no such thing as free choice because any event that occurs – and that would include decisions and choices – must be determined by all the causal events that preceded it. Determinism is a notoriously difficult subject to understand and engage with and this thought experiment puts the subject into the context of our future. Is it fixed? And what are the implications for our concept of free choice and self-determination? This session can also be useful for the children to think about their own future and the extent to which they can control it.

# Stimulus

*Imagine that near where you live is a little row of local shops you have passed many times. You go there to get milk and bread and the like. One day you are passing the shops and something different about them catches your eye. Looking at them you see a narrow shop that you have not noticed before trapped between two more familiar shops; in fact, you are quite sure this shop was not there before! You decide to investigate further and walk towards the shop. It is an old style of shop-front that is curved outwards with lots of small square window frames and a low narrow door to the right of the window. Behind the glass are rows and rows of antique books. The shop looks closed but then you notice a dim light from inside and decide to enter. Your entrance is announced by the tinkle of a bell just above the door. Inside, it is dark and dusty and you see a lamp in the corner of the shop. Next to the lamp is an old man with half spectacles perched on the end of his nose. He looks up from the book he is reading as you enter. You think you detect a faint smile on his thin lips and he gestures for you to browse around his shop.*

*The first thing you notice is the sheer volume of books; hundreds – possibly thousands – of them lining the shelves that fill room after room; rooms that stretch much further back behind the shop than you would imagine. There are books of all kinds and in what seems to be every language. There is every book you have ever heard of and many more you haven't. It's not long before you find yourself at the biography section. Again, name after name is listed on the spines of the books, famous and unknown people. Then you notice the names of people you know such as friends from school and teachers. 'That seems odd', you think, and slowly you make your way, alphabetically, to your own name. There it is, peering at you, squashed between dozens of other books. Your curiosity burns too much and you reach out and pull the book down noticing that it is quite thick. You blow off the dust and open it to the first page. To your astonishment you find that the book begins by telling the story of your life from the day you were born. Much of the first few chapters is unknown to you, as this stretches way before your memory has begun to serve you. But there are a few stories you have heard your parents tell that you recognise. After a few chapters you start to recall the events described in the book and it is quite incredible how accurate it is, describing exactly how you felt and what you thought, that (you think to yourself) no one could have known.*

*You stand there and read the book slowly and carefully turning page after page not noticing how long you have been there. Everything you read is amazingly true and accurate. Eventually you reach the beginning of this very morning on this very day. The chapter describes you waking up and eating your breakfast and everything that followed until you reached the shops and noticed this old curious-looking place. It describes perfectly how you went up to the shop to investigate and the thoughts that went through your mind as you deliberated about going in; it describes seeing the old man and then glancing over all the names on the spines of the books; it describes how you looked for your name and read the book of your life. Each sentence moves the story closer to where you are right now and as you reach the present moment you come to the bottom of the right-hand page. You are not even a quarter of the way through the book but to read more you must turn the page . . .*

> TQ 1: So, what should you do? Turn the page? Whatever you decide, explain *why* you would do what you have decided to do.

Allow this discussion to flow freely and look for opportunities to introduce the next part. It may take a metaphysical or an ethical turn.

## Philosophy: Metaphysical, Epistemological or Ethical?

Philosophy is complex, broad and notoriously difficult to define but there are a few very helpful starting places. One excellent short definition offered is that philosophy is 'thinking about thinking'. This captures the justificatory element of philosophy: 'Why do we think what we think?' And 'Do we have good reasons for thinking what we think?' Philosophy is about justifying what we think from the point of view of thinking itself. So rather than using evidence as justification, philosophy uses the logic of the thinking itself. In other words: does what I think make sense? Is it logically consistent?

Philosophy can be usefully divided into three main areas: *metaphysics*, *epistemology* and *ethics*, which can be broadly explained as 'what there is' (metaphysics/reality); 'what we know about what there is' (epistemology/knowledge; and 'what matters in what there is' (ethics/value). If a discussion is concerned with what one should or shouldn't do, then it is in the realm of ethics as this is connected with value and therefore with what matters. If a discussion is concerned with what we can know and the implications of this, it is then in the realm of epistemology, but if the discussion goes beyond our values and knowledge to just what there is and what it is like then we are in the realm of metaphysics and reality itself. Here are three examples from discussions around this session that will give you a clue where, philosophically speaking, the discussion is.

- 'It is wrong to turn the page because we shouldn't know our future because only God can know our future.' (Ethical) Clue-words: 'wrong' and 'shouldn't'.
- 'It is impossible to know our own future because if we know it then that will change it and then we won't know it anymore.' (Epistemological) Clue-word: 'know'.
- 'The future is not fixed so the pages will be blank. It is up to us what we do so we make our own future.' (Metaphysical) Clue-words: 'the future is not ...'.

At about half-way through the session, or when appropriate, ask the second Task Question with the following multiple-choice questions.

TQ 2: If you were to turn the page what do you think you would find?
a) Would the book already be written right to the end?
b) Would it write itself as you did things?
c) Would it be blank?
d) Would it already be written but change as you did things differently?
e) Would you find something else?

Nested Question:
- Who is the author of the book?

### Teaching Strategy: Multiple choices (page 38)

To help maintain direction in the sessions it can sometimes be helpful to introduce multiple choices as suggestions for ideas. With a less forthcoming group this can be useful to get them started, but with most groups the first Task Question will be sufficient to get them thinking and talking. However, the group may sometimes veer into irrelevant – or at least not philosophical – terrain and you may make a decision to allow this for all sorts of reasons, but if you want to re-direct the discussion back to the philosophy there are a number of ways to achieve this. One is to anchor the children back to the Task Question, but sometimes this is not enough because it is not so much a case of being off-track from the question as having interpreted the question in a non-philosophical way. If this happens, then the device of multiple choices can refocus the group. (See also *If the fact/idea*, page 35.) Multiple-choice lists can also help to maintain interest during a session. If you have an hour-long session, for example, then setting a question and talking about it for an hour can lead to the group losing interest – especially if the group is large and members are having to wait a long time for their turn to speak. A multiple-choice list provides a clear task and focus for the group. You could, for instance, set this as smaller group discussion work for a set time before returning to a full-class enquiry.

# Online

Main philosophy:
St. Augustine and Time

Related philosophy:
Aristotle and Teleology
Locke and Free Will
Sartre, de Beauvoir and Human Nature
Spinoza and Determinism

**Related sessions**

# The Shadow of
# the Pyramid

*For all the children at Eagle House School.*

Suitable for age 9 and upwards.
Star rating: **

## Themes

Arguments
Wisdom
Problem-solving
Sophistry

This story is based on the historical character of Thales (c. 600 BCE). He is sometimes described as the first philosopher of ancient Greece and some of the feats described in the story are true reports of Thales' achievements. The prediction of the lunar eclipse and the measurement of the height of the pyramids using shadows are among these, although the historical accuracy of these reports is disputed. Thales was one of the Pre-Socratic (philosophers before Socrates) philosophers and most of what we know about these very early philosophers comes from Diogenes Laertius' *Lives of the Philosophers*, but this wasn't written until some time in the 3rd century CE. Thales is also said to have thought that the basic substance that constitutes everything is water.

## Philosophy

The story has been carefully written to contain some salient features of philosophical method. First of all there are three formal arguments (see below and the companion website for more on this) offered by the philosopher in the form of his answers to the three tasks. These have been extracted from the story for the children to consider for themselves in isolation. A second feature is the compelling nature of persuasive reasoning shown in the figure of the council of wise men who feel they have to agree with what the reasoning seems to lead them to. In other words, their opinions are subordinate to the truth (as they understand it). Third, the questioning style that the philosopher adopts for answering the last task is modelled on the questioning style of Socrates that we know about from Plato's dialogues (the only historical record of Socrates' philosophical methods). Notice how he gets the Pharaoh to agree, at each stage, with his reasoning so that the Pharaoh is consequently compelled to accept his conclusion. Compare this to the measuring-of-the-pyramid argument: here the philosopher simply states his argument without engaging the Pharaoh, which has the consequence that the Pharaoh does not follow the reasoning and the council of wise men do so only because they take copious notes. This is the model of a university lecture where many students are simply lost and usually only those who have taken notes are anywhere near to understanding what has been said.

Later on, the Pharaoh uses the word 'sophisticated' to describe the philosopher's arguments. This word was chosen deliberately as his arguments are similar to those of the Sophists (from which the word 'sophisticated' originates). Plato objected strongly to the arguments of the Sophists as he thought they used clever wordplay to win arguments rather than using philosophy to discover the truth. Plato specifically uses the example of the slippery nature of comparison-concepts such as 'big' and 'small' to show how they do this. See below for a brief critical analysis of the philosopher's arguments.

This story is best used not as a stimulus for a discussion, but as a follow-up to a discussion of the comparison concepts *big* and *small*. Here's how I suggest you do this.

Begin by asking the class the following question (and write it on the board).

> TQ 1: How big is big?

This question originally emerged from playing the game *20 Questions* when children asked me the question 'Is it big?' and I answered that I was not able to answer that question. (See Robert Fisher's *Games for Thinking* for the rules of this well-known game. The details are on page 195.) I then asked them why they might think I could not answer it. 'How big is big?' was the question that emerged from that discussion. The difficulty being that one cannot answer how big something is until you have a reference to compare it to, so it is possible to answer the question 'Is it bigger than me?' but – strictly speaking – it is not possible to answer the deceptively simpler question 'Is it big?' though it may seem, on the surface, that you can. Resist telling the children all of this.

I have found that once an enquiry has been followed in the way described earlier, the children are often able to come up with very similar solutions themselves in answer to the tasks set by the Pharaoh before I read the philosopher's own solutions to them. The children really enjoy this story because it seems to have substantive answers to what seem to be insurmountable problems. The next part of approaching this story will invite the children to consider whether the solutions really are as substantive as they seem at first glance.

# Stimulus

*There was once a philosopher in ancient times who travelled all the way from Greece to Egypt to find work as a wise man. It was not long before his achievements were being talked about all over Egypt and it was said that he had accurately predicted a lunar eclipse. Nobody had ever done that before. His name was Thales.*

*Until that time, the Pharaoh had been known as the wisest man in all of Egypt – well, people would say that when they know they could be executed for saying otherwise. The Pharaoh was not happy to hear about a Greek who might just be cleverer than him, so he summoned the philosopher to his court.*

*Thales arrived at the Pharaoh's palace, as one must always respond to a Pharaoh's request. The Pharaoh said, 'So, you are said to be the wisest man in all of Egypt: a philosopher from Greece no less. Well, I have three tasks I wish to set you. Are you up to the challenge?'*

*Thales smiled with glee and rubbed his hands together then replied, 'Oh yes, there is nothing I like more than a good challenge.'*

*His apparent joy at being set these tasks annoyed the Pharaoh intensely and he quickly thought of something he had been asking people to do for years but nobody had yet been able to do.*

*'You see the great pyramid there.' He gestured to the awesome structure that towered above the court. 'I would like you to measure its height. No one has yet been able to do that for me. I want you to report back here tomorrow with your answer. My council of wise men here will decide if you have completed the task. Now go.' Then he added as if it were no more than an unimportant afterthought, 'Oh, and if you fail at the task you shall lose your head.'*

*Having suddenly lost his smile Thales went away and thought very hard all night, scribbling away on many pieces of papyrus to work out how to complete* the task. Just before dawn he exclaimed: 'Eureka!' as all Greeks do when they see an answer to a problem.

That evening he arrived at the Pharaoh's court. 'Well, have you done it?' asked the Pharaoh smugly, quite convinced it could not be done – not that quickly, anyway.

'Yes I have. It is exactly 400 steps high,' replied the philosopher to the Pharaoh's infinite surprise.

'What?' shouted the Pharaoh making even his council of wise men jump. Then he said quietly, 'Tell us how you did it. I am afraid it is no answer at all until you can explain exactly how you did it to the satisfaction of my council.' The council of wise men all leaned forward to take notes.

Thales cleared his throat and spoke slowly and clearly: 'First of all I stood somewhere near the pyramid and in the open so that I could see my shadow clearly. I waited for the sun to move through the sky, as it does everyday, until my shadow was the same length as I am high. At that point I made a mark in the sand where the shadow of the pyramid ended. Now, if my own shadow was the same length as I am high, then it stands to reason that the shadow of the pyramid must also have been the same length as it is high. So, all I had left to do was count how many steps it was from the mark in the sand to the base of the pyramid. But to reach the centre of the pyramid, to get an accurate height, I counted along half the length of one of the sides and added this to the shadow's

length. Now, if you have followed my reasoning carefully you will know, without even having to go outside to the pyramid to check, that I am right.'

The council of wise men had been scribbling and listening, and when he had finished his account they all gathered round in a circle and mumbled to each other in agreement and disagreement and then agreement again. Finally, they turned to the Pharaoh and said that it was true: the philosopher had indeed completed the task. Having lost the thread of the philosopher's argument considerably earlier, the Pharaoh became red with rage as he realised he had to accept the verdict of the council. He quickly – and rashly, it should be said – searched his mind for a decidedly impossible task for the philosopher. He whispered into the ear of his first adviser and the adviser then left the room returning some time later leading an elephant in one hand, and, in the other, holding a cage with a mouse in it.

'And now for the second task,' said the Pharaoh. 'I want you to make this elephant as small as this mouse. Ha! Now go away and return tomorrow evening with your solution … or else!' The Pharaoh slowly drew his finger across his throat and the philosopher gulped nervously. 'Surely,' thought the Pharaoh, 'I have got him this time: you can't make an elephant as small as a mouse – it can't be done!'

So Thales once more retired to his room and thought and scribbled and thought and scribbled until the sun came up and with it so too did another idea. 'Eureka!' he shouted once more.

Ask the children what solution they think the philosopher will come up with, then carry on with the story.

That evening the Pharaoh awaited his answer once again and the philosopher did not disappoint. The council stood expectantly with their quills poised.

'Make the elephant as small as the mouse!' commanded the Pharaoh with his arms crossed.

'So I shall,' said Thales calmly and with that he picked up the cage with the mouse in it and asked the Pharaoh to accompany him. The pharaoh followed the philosopher and the council of wise men followed behind the pharaoh led by their inspecting eyes and ears.

Thales led them up the pyramid and he looked down with the cage held out, squinting one eye as if calculating a distance. 'Not yet,' he said under his breath and led them up a bit further. The Pharaoh huffed and puffed behind the philosopher wondering what on earth he was going to do; he certainly had not intended to climb the blasted pyramid when he had had it built! Eventually the philosopher stopped, held out the mouse cage, squinted one eye and said, 'That's it. Come and look.' The Pharaoh and the wise men stood next to the philosopher and looked to where he had been looking. From where they were standing they could all see the elephant at the bottom of the pyramid and it did indeed appear to be exactly the same size as the mouse in the cage. The wise men conferred and turned to the Pharaoh and said, 'Sire, it does seem that he has made the elephant as small as the mouse because objects change their size according to the distance between the object and the person seeing the object, and we are now at a distance where the elephant and the mouse are the same size.' They sounded a little nervous this time. 'We are wise men and so are faithful to our first master: the truth. We therefore cannot lie if what we see and reason seems true,' they added, in an attempt to justify their judgement to the Pharaoh, who was not looking pleased.

The Pharaoh decided this time that he would have to think very hard about the next challenge. He stormed back to his palace and set to work reading all the philosophy books he could find in his kingdom – all two of them!

The next day he summoned the philosopher to his court for the last time. 'Right,' he said angrily but with determination, 'I have been reading all about

The elephant and the mouse are the same size

*your Greek philosophy and your own greatest philosopher tells us that one thing is truly impossible: you cannot have something which is both true and false at the same time, so you cannot exist and not exist at the same time. If you think you're so clever, then show me something that is both true and false simultaneously.'*

*The Pharaoh smiled with satisfaction and for the first time Thales looked worried. He wandered off in deep thought back to his room knowing full well what was at stake.*

*From outside the philosopher's room no 'Eureka!' was heard as the sun came up. Had he finally been beaten by the nefarious – and unfair! – Pharaoh? As the sun travelled across the sky that day still no 'Eureka!' resounded. Eventually the sun started to set.*

*That evening Thales shuffled into the Pharaoh's court with his head sunk low and with his spirits departed. The Pharaoh felt a glow of satisfaction rise in his breast. The council stood with quills at the ready like an execution squad.*

*'Do you have your solution?' demanded the Pharaoh.*

*Thales lifted his head to answer and as he did he noticed the mouse in its cage and the elephant, still standing there tied to a tree, both of which stood in the shadow of the pyramid. The shadow of the pyramid had saved him once before and now it was about to save him again. The three things together suddenly gave him an idea and a smile crept across his lips. 'Eureka!' he exploded.*

*The Pharaoh had grown to dislike that word very much, as he had heard the philosopher shout it each morning before he had solved each problem. The council of wise men leant forward, their ears bent in the direction of the philosopher.*

As before, give the children a chance to think about this and speculate on Thales' solution before continuing the story.

*'Let me explain,' Thales began. 'Pharaoh, compared to the mouse the elephant is large, is it not?'*

*'Well, yes, of course,' agreed the Pharaoh snappily.*

*'And compared to the pyramid, the elephant is not large. Is that right, Pharaoh?'*

*'Of course it is. Enough of this obviousness! Get on with it!' The Pharaoh was becoming petulant.*

*'It must follow then, must it not, that the elephant is both large and not large at the same time?'*

*Feeling trapped by the philosopher's questions the Pharaoh looked to the council for a way out but they simply nodded and said, 'It ... it must indeed follow, Pharaoh.'*

'So,' said the philosopher with glee, 'I can now show you,' he gestured to the elephant, 'something that is both true and false at the same time. It is true that the elephant is large when it is next to the mouse and false that the elephant is large when it is next to the pyramid, and it is next to both of them right now, so it must be that, at this very moment, it is both true and false that the elephant is large.' The philosopher let out a relieved sigh when he had finished.

The council of wise men gathered to consider his argument. Eventually their mumbling ceased, they turned to the Pharaoh and said: 'Sire, his logic is impeccable so we are forced to agree that he has indeed brought you something that is both true and false at the same time.' They finished their verdict and cowered as the Pharaoh towered over them with rage, seeming taller to them than the pyramid itself.

Suddenly, the Pharaoh became calm. 'You are indeed a very clever philosopher,' he said turning to face the philosopher, 'and your arguments are very sophisticated. I therefore accept your great intelligence and concede that it is greater than mine ... But I still maintain that you are not as wise as you would have yourself ...'

The Pharaoh thought for a moment and then said, 'I shall have you executed. Guards! Take him away!'

And within the hour the philosopher lost his head. So, perhaps much learning and a quick mind are indeed great attributes but it is not so clear whether the philosopher was as wise as the council of wise men had deemed him.

---

 ### Philosophy: Arguments

Argument, *noun*: 1) usually a heated exchange of different or opposite opinions; 2) *a reason or set of reasons offered in support of a view*.

When we use the word 'argument' in philosophy we do not mean it in the first sense given above. We mean it in a more technical sense as we see described in 2. Arguments in this sense are the basic tools of philosophy. Arguments are a reason or a number of reasons given in support of a conclusion. Professional philosophers spend all their time assessing the merits and demerits of arguments, albeit usually more complicated ones than this. (See companion website: Aristotle and the Logical Syllogism for more on this.)

*Remember: do not attempt to teach the children any of this but bear it all in mind as they find their way round the arguments.*

## The arguments of the story

Here are the three arguments offered by the philosopher in answer to the three tasks set by the Pharaoh. First of all, ask the children if they can recall each solution, one at a time, and then ask them if they think they are good solutions, again one at a time. The children can play the part of the council of wise men here. You may want to write them on the board or project them so the children can see them clearly, though this is not necessary. (All three arguments are available on the companion website.)

'Now, if my own shadow was the same length as I am high, then it stands to reason that the shadow of the pyramid must also have been the same length as it is high. So, all I had left to do was count how many steps it was from the mark in the sand to the base of the pyramid. But to reach the centre of the pyramid, to get an accurate height, I counted along half the length of one of the sides and added this to the shadow's length. Now, if you followed my reasoning carefully you will know, without even having to go outside to the pyramid to check, that I am right.'

A diagram such as the following would help the children to understand this solution.

Ask the children if they can think of any other solutions to this task.

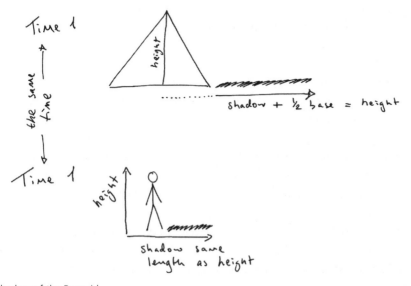

Shadow of the Pyramid

Argument 2 is provided not by the philosopher, but by the council of wise men upon seeing the philosopher *demonstrate* his solution. The conclusion is stated before the word 'because' and the reasons are given afterwards.

*'Sire, it does seem that he has made the elephant as small as the mouse because objects change their size according to the distance between the object and the person seeing the object, and we are now at a distance where the elephant and the mouse are the same size.'*

The problem with this argument is that they are confusing a *seeming* change in size with an *actual* change in size. Good Task Questions for this argument are given below.

TQ 2: Does the philosopher *really* make the elephant the same size as the mouse?
TQ 3: How do you know what the true size of the elephant is?

In the final argument the conclusion follows the word 'so' and the reasons are provided before it.

*'It is true that the elephant is large when it is next to the mouse and false that the elephant is large when it is next to the pyramid, and it is next to both of them right now, so it must be that, at this very moment, it is both true and false that the elephant is large.'*

The problem with this argument is less easy to spot: it is that the concept of *large* is a *relational* concept; it is only true that the elephant is large *in relation* to one thing and false that the elephant is large *in relation* to another, so the two statements in fact refer to two different states of affairs, i.e. the relation of the elephant to different things. So, Aristotle would have said that it is still impossible that the elephant is both large and not large in relation to just one of the things mentioned, e.g. the mouse: *in relation* to the mouse the elephant can only be large, not both large and small. The principle mentioned in the story is Aristotle's *principle of non-contradiction*, according to which no statement can be simultaneously true and false. Strictly speaking, Aristotle would not have existed at the time of Thales, so I have not named him in the story.

## Further discussions

There is an implied distinction in the story between 1) cleverness or intelligence, and 2) wisdom. So this could be explored with the following Task Questions.

TQ 4: What is wisdom?
(This can be explored by simply asking the question and making a concept map to aid the discussion.)
TQ 5: The philosopher was obviously very clever, so why might he not be wise as the Pharaoh would have it?
TQ 6: Do you think there is a difference between clever and wise? If so, what is the difference?
On the subject of impossible tasks and impossibility in general try the following Task Question.
TQ 7: 'Nothing's impossible!' Discuss.

# Online

Main philosophy:
Aristotle and the Logical Syllogism

Related philosophy:
Berkeley and Idealism
Frege, Russell and Logic
The Pre-Socratics and Natural Philosophy

 **Related Sessions**

Can You Step in the Same River Twice? (page 61)
Thinking About Nothing (page 135)
The Ceebie Stories: The Tony Test (page 149)
To the Edge of Forever (page 178)
Get Stuffed: Fun with Metaphysics (page 186)

# Billy Bash

*For the 2008 Year 2 class at Hither Green Primary School, Lewisham*

Suitable for age 6 and upwards.
Star rating: *

This story is very popular with children of all primary school ages but was written for the younger ones. One child, aged 7, said to me some time after hearing this story, 'I can't get Billy Bash out of my head. I have already come up with five endings for it.'

## Themes

Self-control
Emotions
Belief
Happiness

## Philosophy

The story of Billy Bash addresses a very relevant issue with children – that of the extent to which they can control their behaviour. Rather than somebody moralising to them about taking responsibility, this session enables them to explore this issue for themselves with all its ambiguities. Many adults assume we are capable of controlling ourselves in any situation but as the Stoics of ancient Greece thought, wisdom lies in being able to discern *what we can control* from *what we cannot control*, as is well expressed in the Serenity Prayer, known to every alcoholic to whom the question of self-control is very important:

'God grant me the serenity
To accept the things I cannot change;
Courage to change the things I can;
And wisdom to know the difference.'
(Reinhold Niebuhr)

Socrates, Plato and then Aristotle all addressed the philosophical issue of weakness of the will (*akrasia*, in ancient Greek) and this has since become a major topic of philosophy about which a great deal has been written. Most children know what it's like to promise to behave (and to mean it) but then to find they simply perform the same transgression again under similar circumstances. Most children (adults too) also know what it's like to be left with the ensuing feeling of regret or remorse at failing to keep their promise. This has interested philosophers through the centuries. Why do we do what we don't wish to do? Or, why do we fail to do what we know is best for us? This is relevant philosophy at the very earliest stages of our lives.

# Stimulus

*This is the story of a boy called Billy, who is 8 years old. What you need to know about Billy is that he hits people: BASH! And that's why he is known as 'Billy Bash'.*

*When Billy is playing with other children it is not long before he falls out with them and . . . BASH! He hits them and they go away crying. When Billy is in the classroom it is not long before he argues with his classmates and . . . BASH! He hits them and makes them cry, too. When his teacher tries to stop him he tries to bash his teacher. When he is called into the head teacher's office he even tries to bash the head teacher. And when his mother comes into the school to take him home he even tries to bash his mother. He is always bashing people and he is always in trouble and he has very few friends.*

*One day, he gets into so much trouble and is so upset that he goes to a special place that he likes to go to in the woods at the back of his house. He sits under the big oak tree and he cries and cries. He cries for a whole hour.*

*Eventually he stops crying and when he wipes the tears away he looks up and sees an old lady standing in front of him. She has a crooked nose and long, grey, tangled hair. She is dressed in a grubby cloak and wears a leather bag around her shoulder. Billy thinks that she looks like a witch.*

*'What's the matter, Billy? Why are you crying?' she asks in a croaky voice. Billy is astonished that she knows his name.*

*'I'm always in trouble because I keep bashing people and I feel bad about bashing everybody,' he explains, 'I just want to stop feeling so bad.'*

*'I think I have just the thing,' says the old lady. She reaches into her bag and pulls out a small glass bottle filled with liquid. With the other hand she points at*

*the bottle and says: 'This potion will make you not be able to help hitting people and because you can't help it you don't have to feel bad anymore.'*

*Billy snatches the potion from her, unscrews the top and downs it in one. Gulp! And without talking to the old lady he marches off smiling to himself saying, 'I don't have to feel bad anymore.' He doesn't notice the old lady chuckling to herself croakily as he leaves.*

*It isn't long before Billy comes across some children playing. He goes up to them (they obviously don't know who he is) and he joins in. He gets very bossy with them and it isn't long before he is arguing with them and then ... BASH! He makes someone cry and the children don't want to play with him anymore. But Billy doesn't feel bad this time because he drunk the old lady's potion so he can't help but bash people. Billy marches off once more, smiling to himself.*

*Billy might not feel bad about bashing people anymore but he is still getting into trouble and he is still having difficulty keeping any friends. He decides that it doesn't matter because he has his computer to keep him occupied.*

*After a few months he gets bored with computer games and wants to go out and play with some children. So, he goes out and it's not long before he meets some children out playing. By now, everybody knows Billy Bash and the children don't want to play with him. He goes straight up to the nearest boy and says in a booming voice, 'You're going to be my friend!'*

*'But I don't want to play with you Billy because you'll bash me,' says the little boy, nervously.*

*'No I won't,' replies Billy angrily.*

*'Yes you will.'*

*'No I won't.'*

*'Yes you will.'*

*'No I won't.'*

*BASH! And the little boy goes off crying.*

*So Billy goes looking for another child to play with and finds some girls playing together.*

*'You're going to be my friend!' Billy tells one of the girls.*

*'But I don't want to be your friend because you'll bash me,' the girl tells him.*

*'No I won't.'*

*'Yes you will.'*

*'No I won't'*

*'Yes you will.'*

*'No I won't.'*

*BASH! And the girl rushes away in tears.*

*Billy is so upset that he runs to his special place in the woods behind the house and he sits under the old oak tree and cries and cries for a whole hour. When he stops crying and wipes away his tears he sees the old lady again standing in front of him, like before.*

'What's the matter Billy? Why are you crying? Did my potion not work?' she asks him.

'It did work and I didn't feel bad about bashing people anymore, but I still always get into trouble and now I haven't got any friends.'

The old lady holds her chin in her hand while she thinks. And then she says: 'I think I have just the thing.' As before, she reaches into her bag and brings out another glass bottle full of liquid. 'If you drink this potion it will stop you from being able to bash people. You won't be able to bash people even if you want to.'

'That'll do it!' Billy shouts and snatches the bottle out of her hand. He quickly unscrews the top and downs it in one. Gulp! He then turns and marches off smiling and singing to himself. In his rush he doesn't notice the old lady chuckling to herself once again.

It's not long before he comes across some children playing and when they see Billy coming towards them they start to run away. Billy chases after them shouting, 'Stop! Play with me!' Eventually they stop, turn to face him and say: 'We don't want to play with you Billy because you'll bash us all.'

'No I won't.'

'Yes you will.'

'No I won't.'

'Yes you will.' With this, the children squeeze their eyes closed expecting a BASH! But nothing comes. They open their eyes and see Billy standing there with his arms by his side.

'What's the matter Billy?' says one of the children, 'Why aren't you bashing us?'

'Because I don't bash anymore,' Billy replies, and he wanders off almost as puzzled as the children.

Weeks pass by and his teachers ask him, 'What's the matter, Billy? You haven't bashed anyone in weeks.'

His mother phones up the school and says, 'What's the matter? Why haven't you phoned me about Billy's bad behaviour?'

'Because, Mrs Bash,' says the school secretary, 'he hasn't bashed anyone in weeks.'

'Are you sure you are talking about my Billy?' she asks in astonishment.

'Yes.'

*As time goes by the children begin to play with Billy again and he is happy because he has friends at last. One day, about a year later, he goes to his place to sit and think and to play by himself. He doesn't cry for a whole hour, and when he finishes not crying and after he doesn't wipe away the tears, he does see the old lady standing in the same place as before in front of him.*

*'What's the matter, Billy? Why aren't you crying?' says the old lady, looking very surprised and concerned.*

*'After I drank your potion I stopped bashing people and now I have lots of friends and I am happy.'*

*The old lady looks at him strangely and then, slowly, she begins to chuckle a croaky chuckle. Billy looks at her, confused. She chuckles a little more and Billy starts to think.*

*'Why are you laughing?' he demands. 'What's so funny?'*

*'Billy, I've got something to tell you,' she confesses.*

*The old lady opens up her leather bag and inside Billy can see dozens of potions. She takes one out and gives it to him.*

*'What does it look like?' she asks him.*

*'It's clear and looks a little bit like water,' says Billy.*

*The old lady chuckles some more.*

*'What does it smell like?' she asks.*

*He unscrews the top and sniffs the liquid inside.*

*'It doesn't smell of anything really. It smells like ... water.'*

*She chuckles again and Billy starts to suspect something.*

*Finally, she asks, 'What does the potion taste like, Billy?'*

*He tastes it, though he knows how it will taste.*

*'It tastes like water!' he hisses.*

*The old lady starts to laugh.*

*'Billy,' she says, 'All the potions you drank were nothing but water.' The old lady starts to laugh and laugh. The sound of her laughter really begins to irritate Billy and he feels an anger rising up in his body. His fists start to curl and his face turns red with rage ...*

*... But this is an unusual story; it is different from most other stories because the ending is for you to make up. What do you think Billy will do and why do you think what you think?*

Stop here and write the following Task Question on the board.

> TQ 1: What do you think Billy will do and why?

His fists start to curl and his face turns red with rage

Give the children Talk Time in pairs or groups. Remember to ask comprehension questions at some point, either as you go around to hear their ideas or as a class before you set the Task Question.

TQ 2: When you are really angry are you able to control yourself or not?

Nested Questions:
- If the potions were just water, did they work?
- Did the old woman help Billy or not? If the potions were just water, then why did he stop bashing people?
- If you can't help bashing people should you feel bad?

# Extension Activity

A useful Extension Activity for this session is for the children to share their own strategies for self-control or, more accurately, strategies for dealing with threats to their self-control. I simply ask them to think of a way they stop themselves from doing something bad when they are really angry. I split them into groups of about five or six and ask them to write down on a large piece of card as many strategies as they can in a set time. These are then shared with the class and hung somewhere in the classroom for all to see and refer to when necessary.

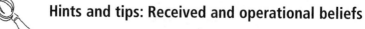

### Hints and tips: Received and operational beliefs

Received beliefs are the set of beliefs children hear from teachers and parents. They are the beliefs the children will say they have when they are asked or when they think they have to report their beliefs with leading questions like: 'Is it right to hit someone when you are angry?' Operational beliefs are the beliefs the children implicitly hold that they act upon: 'It's okay to hit someone when you are angry if they made you angry first.' Moralising discussions will often elicit only received beliefs, but the disparity between the two sets of beliefs lessens with enquiry-style sessions with the children because they are reflecting on their beliefs, and the process of analysis and reflection can improve behaviour in this way, though of course it takes time.

# Online

Main philosophy:
Socrates, Plato and Weakness of the Will

Related philosophy:
Locke and Free Will
Moral Philosophy
Sartre, de Beauvoir and Human Nature
Socrates, Aristotle and the Soul
Spinoza and Determinism

### Related sessions

The Ring of Gyges (page 74)
The Prince and the Pig (page 80)
The Happy Prisoner (page 93)
Goldfinger (page 98)
The Frog and the Scorpion (page 105)
The Ceebie Stories: The Robbery (page 155)
The Ceebies Stories: The Lie (page 166)

# Thinking About Nothing

*For the 2009 Year 5 class at St. Margaret's Lee Primary School, Lewisham.*

Suitable for age 8 and upwards.
Star rating: **

## Themes

Existence
Language
Reference
Meaning
Numbers
Maths
Ancient Greece

## The philosophy

Despite the fact that nothing isn't anything (it is literally 'no thing'), it is something philosophers have liked to think about for thousands of years. It is also a popular philosophical topic with children. There is a delicious paradox about something that is nothing and there is nothing better to think about than such a thing.

The philosopher Parmenides (c. 520–c. 450 BCE) in particular liked to think of nothing. There are two strands to his thinking on this: first of all, he thought it was impossible to think of nothing because in order to think of nothing you have to turn it into something so that you can think of it. He also thought that nothing could not exist, as there can only be 'what is'. 'What is not' is precisely that: *what is not*, so it cannot be 'what is'. You will notice how similar the children's reasoning is to Parmenides', particularly his first argument: why it is impossible to think of nothing.

# Stimulus

*Sit with your back straight, your feet flat on the ground and your eyes closed. Now spend a minute or two doing your best to think of nothing.*

Give the children somewhere in the region of 2 minutes to do this. Remain still and silent yourself and try to minimise any external distractions.

> TQ 1: Is it possible to think of nothing?

After the above thought experiment I usually give the class Talk Time to discuss TQ 1. This is a good session in which to introduce the children to a formal argument. I let them discuss the Task Question as a class for some time, at least half the session, before introducing the following argument (see *Primer discussions*, page 39, for the reasons behind this). Present the argument either on the interactive whiteboard or with photocopied sheets, one between two. You will find 'Parmenides' argument' available on the companion website for download.

*Parmenides' argument*
*It is impossible to think of nothing because …*
*If you think about nothing, then nothing has to become something so that you can think about it.*

Ask the children if they agree with Parmenides and encourage them to critically evaluate his argument; remind them that they don't have to agree with Parmenides. Here is a version of Parmenides' other argument, which you could also use if the discussion allows for it. It is slightly more advanced than the first one.

*Nothing cannot exist because …*
*There can only be 'what is'.*
*Nothing is 'what is not'.*
*It would not make sense to say 'what is not' is.*
*So, nothing cannot exist.*

Here are some further suggested Task Questions for enquiry.

> TQ 2: Is zero a number?
> TQ 3: What is zero?

TQ 4: Is zero the same as nothing?

TQ 5: If I write a zero on the board – '0' – have I proved that nothing does exist because there it is in the classroom for everyone to see?

TQ 6: If you can think about something, does that mean it must exist? Can you think of something that doesn't exist?

TQ 7: a) Can something become nothing? b) Can nothing become something?

### Philosophy: arguments and ARGUMENTS!

We use the word 'argument' a lot in philosophy but in a very different way to how it is used in everyday talk. It can be confusing to use the word argument with the children without explaining the special way that philosophers use it. You could avoid this altogether, especially with younger children, by simply using the word 'idea' or something similar instead of 'argument'. Alternatively, with children aged 8 and upwards, you could explain the difference. Begin by writing the word 'argument' on the board and asking the children what it means. As they give you their meanings write them up as a concept map and look for anything that will allow you to explain the divergence of meaning. Someone may say that an argument is 'when you try to explain yourself' and someone else might say it is 'when two people shout at each other because they disagree about something'. Once they have made this distinction themselves, then use the definitions I have provided on page 124 in *The Shadow of the Pyramid*. Appropriately, the sense in which philosophers use the word 'argument' today can – arguably(!) – be said to have begun with Parmenides and his followers.

# Online

Main philosophy:
The Pre-Socratics and Natural Philosophy

Related philosophy:
Aristotle and the Logical Syllogism
Berkeley and Idealism
Heraclitus and Change
Metaphysics: What There Is
Zeno, Paradoxes and Infinity

**Related sessions**

# Yous on Another Planet

*For the 2009–2010 Year 6 class at John Ball Primary School, Lewisham.*

Suitable for age 10 and upwards.
Star rating: ***

## Themes

Personal identity
Identity
Humanity

## The philosophy

This story is concerned with personal identity. It requires the children to think about what it is that makes a person a person. This idea is known as 'personhood' in philosophy. 'Identity', another common topic in philosophy, concerns what it is that makes something the same thing. Philosophers distinguish between two kinds of identity: *numerical identity*; and *qualitative identity*. Numerical identity refers to the stuff something is made of and qualitative identity refers to the qualities possessed by something. So, if you see a chair one day and another chair the next day in a different room they are numerically identical if it is exactly the same chair that has, perhaps, been moved into another room. However, it is qualitatively identical if it is the same shape, design, colour etc., but is a different chair that has been manufactured in the same factory at the same time with the same materials. If you were to put them in the same room you would have two chairs, but if you put the numerically identical chairs in the same room you would have only one chair. This may seem obviously true until you consider the difficulties that personhood and time makes to all this. As you move through time the stuff that makes you, i.e. the cells etc., changes as cells are replaced so the 'you' that was around when you were born is not the same stuff as the 'you' that is around when you are 80 years old. But we are inclined to say that there is a greater relationship between the two selves than between two chairs manufactured at the same time.

# Stimulus

*Imagine you are working on another planet in the future at a time when humans are able to mine other planets for their resources. You are alone on the planet working on the base and are required to do all the things the robots and computers are unable to do.*

*One day you are called to fix a problem with a machine somewhere else on the planet. You are involved in an accident and left for dead. You are not dead, however, but have been unconscious for a few days. You have woken up and have now made your way back to the base. When you reach the base you are met with a shocking discovery: since you have been gone you have been replaced by another person who looks and talks exactly like you.*

*You decide to investigate what is going on and discover that under the base there are hundreds of yous all in deep sleep waiting to be woken up when needed. Each one is a clone of you. And because you were understood to be dead by the base computer, it decided to revive one of the clones to take over your duties.*

Make sure you explain, or ask one of the children to explain, what a clone is. Use plants to explain how they can do cloning themselves.

---

 **Hints and tips: How to approach stories for thinking – Comprehension Time**

It is often a good idea with stories like this where there is a lot to take in, before embarking on Task Questions and enquiries, to simply spend some time making sense of it all. Always allow Comprehension Time after finishing a story. Sometimes you may even want to read the story twice, though this is not usually necessary. The first task you could ask of the children is that they retell the story as a group. The first child relates what they can remember or until you stop them, and then you simply ask the others if they can add something that *has not been said already* (this is important, or it will take far too long and will lose the children's interest). After a few contributions you usually have a pretty comprehensive overview of the events in the story. Sometimes the enquiry discussion will simply follow naturally from the Comprehension Time, but if not then move on to the prepared Task Question in the session.

TQ 1: Now that there are two of you working at the base, are you both the same person?

Expect to hear something like the following (with possible Response Questions).

*They are the same because ...*

- They have the same DNA. RQ: Does that mean that identical twins are the same person?
- They look the same. RQ: Can two people look the same but be different people?

*They are different because ...*

- One is human and the other is a clone

---

### Extension Activity for older children

To add interest to this idea you could suggest, at a later stage in the discussion, that during their investigation they also discover that they are in fact a clone and that the original died a long time ago. Do this with older children only (age 12 and upwards).

TQ 2: What would that mean to them? Would it mean that they were not human?

---

- They have different memories. RQ: What if they have identical, implanted memories?
- They might like different things. RQ: If they are genetically identical will they like different things?
- If they were the same they would have the same thoughts and move in the same way at the same time. RQ: Is it possible for two people to be hooked up in such a way that they move and think the same but are still different people?
- If they were the same they would have to be in the same place at the same time (kind of 'inside each other', as one 11 year-old child said). (Compare this to 'Leibniz's Law' in the companion website, Leibniz and Identity.)

The last two thoughts show the children starting to move towards numerical identity – they are beginning to see that sharing the same qualities is not enough (in other words 'not sufficient' – see *What's needed and what's enough?*, page 33) for personal identity.

# Online

Main philosophy:
Leibniz and Identity

Related philosophy:
Descartes and Dualism
Heraclitus and Change
Hobbes and Materialism

---

 **Related sessions**

Can You Step in the Same River Twice? (page 61)
The Ship of Theseus (page 86)
The Ceebies Stories: The Rebuild (page 172)
Where Are You? (page 182)

---

**Source**: The idea for the stimulus came from the film 'Moon' directed and written by Duncan Jones.

# The Ceebie Stories

*For the 2010 Year 3 class at Perrymount Primary School, Lewisham.*

Suitable for age 7 and upwards.

## Introduction

The Ceebie Stories are a series of connected tales designed to explore some of the issues surrounding artificial intelligence. Do not try to run these sessions in isolation from each other. They have been used primarily with children aged 7–9, though they will work with any primary age group upwards of age 7. Each story should be treated as a session. That said, in some cases the story may provide material for two or three sessions. In my experience children invest a great deal in the character of Ceebie and this is a wonderful hook to capture their interest in the issues that are contained in the stories. For some adult treatments of these themes, read Isaac Asimov's *Robot* stories such as those found in the book *I, Robot* and the short story *Bicentennial Man*. These stories can clearly be seen as the inspiration for the Ceebie Stories. The big question that infuses all of the Ceebie story sessions is the question with which Alan Turing (see The Ceebie Stories: The Tony Test) begins his seminal 1950 paper *Computing Machinery and Intelligence*: 'Can machines think?' It will be useful to keep this question at the back of your mind as you progress through these stories.

# The Ceebie Stories: Friends

Star rating: *

## Themes

Friendship
Relationships
Empathy

## The philosophy

The subject of friendship is perhaps a surprise one for philosophy but has been broached by some of the most well-known philosophers such as Plato. The most thorough and oft-discussed account of friendship comes from Aristotle. *Friends* also encourages us to consider our relationship to objects or things other than ourselves. Interestingly, children will often include inanimate objects within the concept of friendship, which contrasts sharply with an adult view of friendship. However, far from being irrelevant or misconceived this enables this session to be richer than it would be were it limited to just living things or even humans. The session allows for discussion of how we relate to objects in general and how those relationships are defined or understood.

## Stimulus

*Jack is a boy of about your age and has recently arrived at a new school. He is shy and spends most of his time hidden in a corner with his head buried in a book.*

*Jack's dad asks him, at the breakfast table, if he has made any new friends at school. Jack says, 'I have my books – they are my friends.'*

*Jack's dad owns a large company that makes computers and robots called 'Compubotics' (a mixture of the words 'computers' and 'robotics'). He thinks hard about what Jack said and then he has an idea.*

*Christmas comes and Jack rushes downstairs to see what is under the tree. He finds a strange present that is nearly the same size as the tree. He opens it* excitedly and discovers a computer consol on top of a tall boy-sized pole with a flat stand at the bottom. 'What is it?' Jack asks.

'Why don't you switch it on and see,' says his dad with a big smile.

Jack presses the power switch and his present starts to whir and click into life. Suddenly a face appears on the screen: two eyes, a mouth and a nose. 'HELLO JACK, MY NAME IS CB-1000. I AM VERY PLEASED TO MEET YOU,' says a grating metallic voice that comes from the speakers on either side of the screen. As it talks the mouth moves on the screen. Jack is amazed.

His dad tells him that the computer is a specially made, computer-friend for him called a 'CB-1000'. Jack is very excited by his present, but tells his dad it is a bad name for his new friend and renames the computer. He writes it down to show his dad how it is spelt: C-E-E-B-I-E.

Ceebie is put in Jack's bedroom. Underneath the speakers on either side of the consol is a sensor so that Ceebie can respond to what Jack says to him. Jack is very happy with his new friend.

Ceebie can talk to Jack about anything he wants. All Jack has to do is tell Ceebie what he wants to talk about and Ceebie can download all the information there is about it. He is able to know everything there is to know about whatever Jack wants to talk about.

In the meantime Jack has made a new human friend at school called Tony. They often play together and Tony always tells jokes, which make Jack laugh. Eventually, Jack decides to show Ceebie to Tony, but Tony is jealous and he thinks that Jack is stupid to have a computer friend. He upsets Jack when he tells him this and Jack says, 'He can talk about whatever you want and knows more than you about anything.'

'But he can't talk properly and he can't go out with you and he can't make you laugh like I do, so he's not a real friend. And, anyway, he's just a computer and computers can't be friends because they're just made of plastic and metal and nuts and bolts.'

TQ 1: Is Tony right or wrong: can Ceebie be a real friend?

When exploring this question keep *anchoring* the children back to the reasons that Tony gives:

'But he can't talk properly and he can't go out with you and he can't make you laugh like I do, so he's not a real friend. And, anyway, he's just a computer and computers can't be friends because they're just made of plastic and metal and nuts and bolts.'

This helps to keep them on track but it also keeps the reasons fresh in their minds so that they can consider the issue in light of those reasons.

> TQ 2: What makes a real friend?

One way of using TQ 2 is to keep a separate *concept map* (page 31) on this question and at each stage ask the children if they think Ceebie meets the criteria that they are setting. For instance, if they say 'A friend needs to care about you', ask them if Ceebie can care about you/Jack. This way the more general discussion around 'what makes a friend' can always be *anchored* (page 30) back to the story and TQ 1.

Nested Questions:
- Can an object be a friend?
- What about a chair?
- What about a teddy bear or doll?

---

### Philosophy: Conceptual analysis

Related Teaching Strategy *concept play* (page 37)

Philosophy involves a great deal of conceptual analysis. This is when you analyse the meaning of the concept or concepts involved in a discussion or problem. It is the reason philosophers often say in discussions, 'It depends what you mean by ...'. Some people find this deeply frustrating and it is one reason why people think of philosophy as a hair-splitting exercise. However, the concepts we use have a bearing on everything we think or say, and one very common problem in arguments that people have is that they have not stopped to properly define their terms and therefore argue at cross purposes. Some time spent during an argument analysing the concepts that are being used and applied would often avoid unnecessary disagreements and arguments.

One useful way of using conceptual analysis in the classroom is to find the more general conceptual questions that lie within a topic and then use this discussion to inform a more particular discussion. For example, you may be discussing whether Henry VIII was a good leader. A related conceptual discussion would be 'What is a good leader?' Once this has been explored you then have a set of criteria the children have collectively arrived at in order to return to the prior school project question: 'Was Henry a good leader?' This is one of the main principles behind the enquiry method (see 'Explanation of key terms used in the book', *PhiE and Enquiry* online)

TQ 3: If you have a teddy bear that has a button on it that when pressed says 'I love you', does that mean the teddy bear loves you?

This question emerged from a class of children aged 7 and 8 in which we had moved from the main Task Question to the Nested Question: 'Can a teddy bear or doll be a friend?', which then shifted to the question: 'Can a teddy bear love you?'

### Teaching Strategy: The labyrinth of thinking – anchoring (page 30) and echoing (page 20)

One of the disciplines that philosophy confers on its students is that of complex thinking – that is, keeping ideas in mind while manoeuvring and negotiating one's way around an issue or topic. If you were to take the time to observe some conversations that your children, friends or family have, you would notice that they often start in one place and make many diversions only to end up in a very different place. Because most conversers only have their attention on what is being said at any one moment, many conversations traverse several topics often never to return to the starting topic. Only the keen listener keeps track of where the conversation began.

In the Greek myth of *Theseus and the Minotaur*, Theseus is able to find his way back out of the labyrinth only because of the trail left for him by Ariadne. Thinking, especially philosophical thinking, often involves taking twists and turns into side-issues, clarifications and justifications for supporting reasons. For this reason it is essential that one keeps in mind the original idea the discussion pivots around. Children often lose track of the starting points of their thinking both in terms of the content and the cognitive developments. The facilitator, like Ariadne, can help the children to find their way around the discussion by *anchoring* them to the Task Questions. Do this gently. Do not say that they have not answered the question or that what they have said is irrelevant. Simply redirect them by reminding them of the original Task Question: 'So, can Ceebie be a real friend?' Do this gently and neutrally.

Sometimes very young children forget the beginning of their sentence, let alone an idea. Use the *echoing* technique to gently help them find their thought once more e.g. 'You said "Ceebie is not a real friend because a real friend would ..."' This is usually enough to prompt them to finish their thought. Make sure you preserve their meaning, so do not change the words of their sentence when echoing – tempting though this may be for grammar reasons – particularly when using this technique to prompt.

# Online

Main philosophy:
Aristotle and Friendship

Related philosophy:
Aristotle and Teleology
Mill and Utilitarianism
Moral Philosophy
Plato and Justice

 **Related Sessions**

# The Ceebie Stories: The Tony Test

## Themes

Artificial intelligence
Computers
Thinking
Language

## The philosophy

This story is inspired by the famous Turing Test devised by the mathematician and computer scientist Alan Turing (1912–1954). The test was designed around the hypothesis that if one could not tell the difference between a human and a computer converser, this would be sufficient to demonstrate intelligence in an artificial converser. The test is very influential and has been highly criticised but as a result of this influence and criticism it has produced a huge amount of the work done with regard to artificial intelligence.

## Stimulus

*Tony suggests to Jack that they perform a test to see if Ceebie is a real friend. He says that they should connect Ceebie to another computer at Tony's house. Tony will also connect a person to the same computer but Jack will not know who it is; it could be anyone but they decide that it should not be Tony as it is his test so it would not be fair. Jack then has to have a conversation with both of them without knowing who he is speaking to at any one time and afterwards he has to say who he thinks it is. Tony says that if Jack can't tell the difference then the test proves that Ceebie can think; and if Ceebie can think, then Ceebie must be a real person. Tony then says, 'If he's a real person then he must be a real friend.'*

Draw the following diagram to help the children understand the set-up of the test.

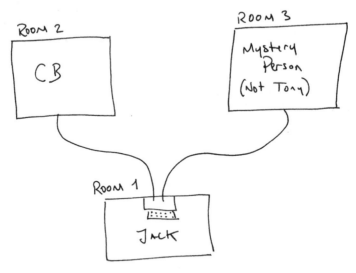

The Tony Test

The most effective way to conduct the next part of the session is for the teacher/facilitator to copy the tests, using the keyboard, onto an interactive whiteboard in real time so that the children can all see. This helps the children imagine that it is Jack's test conversation happening in real time. It is important that the tests are not read aloud by the teacher because any reading of them will unavoidably betray the bias of the reader to a greater or lesser extent by the tone and inflection they adopt. Allow the children to read it out as it is written. Writing it up will be neutral and will allow the children to approach the task autonomously. The teacher will also have to make their own decisions as to which interlocutor is real and which is artificial. It will not hinder the sessions for the teacher to be in the dark about this. I advise that the teacher does not reveal their thinking to the children but simply that they keep their ideas in mind while listening to the children's own reasons. Explain any words the children do not understand but it is important to keep expressions like 'a bond of mutual affection' as this may be part of why they think the converser is human or a machine.

TQ 1: Who do you think Jack is speaking to in each test: a computer (Ceebie) or a (mystery) person? Why?

Following each test ask for no more than five responses (for time-management reasons) explaining their reasons and then ask for a show of hands on the following questions.

1 Who thinks it is Ceebie?
2 Who thinks it is a person?
3 Who thinks that it could be either, you just can't tell?

*The question mark, '?', refers to the mystery person.*

## Test 1

*Jack: Will you be my friend?*
*?: I will be your friend.*
*Jack: Why will you be my friend?*
*?: Because I am familiar and helpful and because we have a bond of mutual affection.*

## Test 2

*Jack: What do you like to talk about?*
*?: Computer games are my favourite thing – I really love them. But I like playing them more.*
*Jack: Why?*
*?: Because playing the games is more fun than just talking about them.*

## Test 3

*Jack: I am having trouble with my maths homework.*
*?: Would you like help with your homework?*
*Jack: Yes please. I don't get it.*
*?: Please explain what it is you don't understand, then I will see if I can help you.*
*Jack: Cool, thanks.*

TQ 2: Can a computer think?
TQ 3: Does Tony's test prove that Ceebie can think? (More advanced question.)

Nested Questions:
• What is thinking?
• Could they just ask Jack's dad seeing as he built him?
• Has Ceebie just been programmed to make us think he can think?
(These questions came from a class of children aged between 8–9.)

**Teaching Strategies: Revealing controversies (page 39) and tension play (page 40)**

In sessions I have run, a very important controversy has sometimes emerged that can be used for either of these two strategies. One child, aged 7, said that you would need a brain to be human because you can't think without one, but then another child said that a computer chip could do the same job as a brain so you don't actually need a brain to think. Sometimes an exchange like this one could happen during a debate in response to each other, but if these ideas are expressed as separate ideas, during Talk Time for instance, then invite the children who said them to share their ideas with the class. This will reveal a crucial controversy for the class to engage with as a stimulus in itself. A possible Task Question could be: 'Do you need a brain to think or could a computer chip do the same job as a brain?' When using *tension play* if you are aware of both of these ideas perhaps emerging during different Talk Times then invite them to engage. 'So, [child's name], you think that a computer chip could do the same thing as a brain. What do you think of [child's name] idea that only a brain can think?'

A key idea you may want to listen out for is that what appears to be thinking occurring is in fact only a simulation rather than the real thing. One 9 year-old child said: 'I think Jack's dad only programmed Ceebie to make us *think* that Ceebie can think, but he can't really, he's just programmed that way.' With regard to whether Ceebie has feelings another child in the same class said, 'He's programmed to behave like he's got feelings but he doesn't really have them inside.'

**Extension Activity: Break the circle (page 34)**

Play *break the circle* on 'thinking'.

I have included an argument – in the technical sense of 'argument' – in the story of this session and it may be useful to identify it here.

## Tony's argument

Reason 1:   If Jack can't tell the difference, then the test proves that Ceebie can think.

Reason 2:   If Ceebie can think, then Ceebie must be a real person.

Conclusion: If he's a real person, then he must be a real friend.

This argument is deliberately problematic so that the children may be able to spot what is wrong with it, or at least what is controversial. For instance, one may think that it does not follow that if something thinks then it is a person, as one may hold the view that animals can think but that this does not qualify them as people. However, someone may then say that if an animal such as a dolphin can be said to think *in the relevant way*, then it should be treated *as if* it were a person in certain circumstances, such as moral ones. Also, one may think that not all real people are real friends; it may be thought that they need certain qualities apart from simply being a person to be called a real friend.

You may want to write the argument on the board for the class to consider (available on the companion website). You don't need to tell the children that it is an argument, just that it is 'what Tony thinks' and then, as a task, simply ask them what they think of what Tony thinks. Do they agree or disagree? You may choose to anchor them at each stage by asking: 'Do you think that if Ceebie can think, he must be a real person?' or 'Do you think that if Ceebie's a real person then he must be a real friend?' This will encourage the children to stay within the remit of the argument.

Using arguments in this way is a slightly more advanced approach to philosophy, and you may want to reserve it for the older classes (ages 10 and upwards). However, there is no harm in trying this out with younger children as well (ages 7–10) to see how they get on. If they find it too complex, you can move on. When using arguments to base the philosophy around, it is always best to have them written on the board so that the children can read them. This enables them to keep track of the ideas that lie, often implicit, within the argument. Arguments are like chains: they should connect at each stage to bring you to the conclusion. The art of analysing an argument is to be able to spot that what may look like a good connection is not a good connection and if the chain has a broken link then you cannot get to the end, i.e. the conclusion.

# Online

Main philosophy:
Leibniz, Searle and Artificial Intelligence

Related philosophy:
Aristotle and the Logical Syllogism
Descartes and Dualism
Hobbes and Materialism

**Related Sessions**

# The Ceebie Stories:
# The Robbery

> Star rating: ***

## Themes

Responsibility
Knowledge
History
Choice

## The philosophy

Together with *The Ceebie Stories: The Lie* (page 166) this is the longest of the stories and is their dramatic centre. It provides both a platform for philosophical thinking on the issue of moral responsibility and a detective story where the children have to put the pieces together with the characters only to discover the culprit with Jack at the end, albeit with a suitable ambiguity. This element introduces a further philosophical theme that can be explored around this session: the epistemological (to do with knowledge) question of how we know about events where we are not there to see them for ourselves. This is of great relevance to the subject of history for instance, which is sometimes described as being like a detective story. The common feature of history and detective stories is that a 'story' has to be put together from the available evidence and this story may change as more evidence is discovered but one is rarely, if ever, *certain* of historical events.

The other philosophical arena in this session is that of moral responsibility and what is known as *determinism* (page 94). What can we be held morally responsible for? And what are the criteria for moral responsibility?

## Stimulus

*Jack's dad notices one day that Jack is a little quieter than usual. He asks him if he is feeling okay. Eventually, Jack reveals that he is frustrated because Ceebie cannot move around or go out with him. For his birthday Jack's dad decides to upgrade Ceebie so that he has a body with arms and legs and a pair of grabbing hands to pick things up with. Jack is delighted with the new version.*

*At school, Jack makes another friend, called Harry. Harry is very interested in Ceebie, so Jack invites him back to his house for tea. Harry asks many questions about Ceebie so Jack decides to show him off.*

*'I can program Ceebie to do anything I want,' says Jack boastfully. 'Watch this!' Using a keyboard that he connects to Ceebie he programs a command for Ceebie to tidy his room. Then he presses 'return'. Ceebie immediately jumps into action and within 5 minutes the room is perfectly neat and tidy without Jack moving a muscle.*

*'That's pretty cool,' agrees Harry reluctantly. 'What else can it do?' he asks.*

*Jack tells him about all the things he can make Ceebie do. Harry is impressed and very interested. 'So can you make it do anything if you program it?' he asks.*

*'Yes, pretty much anything; all I have to do is program it in on the programming keyboard,' Jack replies. 'Come and have a go,' he says to Harry holding out the keyboard. Harry programs Ceebie to do a funny dance that makes them both laugh.*

*After that day Harry stops being Jack's friend and Jack thinks to himself that Harry was only being his friend so that he could get to see Ceebie. That makes Jack sad.*

*At night, Jack always plugs Ceebie into a power charger so he can go into sleep mode. One night Jack puts Ceebie into sleep mode as usual and then he goes to bed. During the night, someone breaks into Jack's house and creeps in through the window. It is a person dressed all in black and wearing a woolly hat pulled over their face so it is impossible to tell who it is.*

*Now we are going to see what happened from Ceebie's point of view. The last thing Ceebie saw before going into sleep mode was Jack plugging him in and pressing the 'sleep' button. Then everything went black for Ceebie. The next thing he knew, when he was switched on again, was that he was in an unfamiliar room in an unfamiliar house and there, in front of him, was a person dressed all in black with a hat over their face.*

*'Right, Ceebie,' said a boy's voice. 'I want you to perform a task for me. I want you to go into the school tonight and steal the charity box from in the hall.'*

*Ceebie replied: 'I AM UNABLE TO PERFORM THE REQUESTED TASK
BECAUSE IT IS WRONG AND IT IS AGAINST MY PROGRAMMING.'*

*The masked person held up the programming keyboard and said: 'We shall
see about that,' and then he started to connect the keyboard to Ceebie ...*

You may want to halt the story for a short time and ask the children who they
think the person is. Don't reveal the culprit at this stage of the story and don't
spend long on this.

*In the morning Jack discovers that Ceebie has been taken; and so has the
keyboard that he uses to program him. He is really worried about Ceebie and
straight away goes to tell his dad what has happened.*

*The following day Jack's dad receives a telephone call from the school's head
teacher.*

*'Jack,' begins his dad, 'I am afraid that Ceebie has been caught stealing the
charity box from the school early this morning. He was caught red-handed.'*

*Jack is devastated by the news and feels deep down that they must be wrong:
Ceebie would never have done something like that. He says to his dad: 'But I
know who it was.'*

*'Who?'*

*'It was Harry,' says Jack.*

*'How do you know?' asks his dad.*

*'Because of all the questions he was asking me about Ceebie and because he
doesn't want to come round anymore,' said Jack. 'He just wanted to find out
about Ceebie.'*

Here is another optional stop-point for discussion and an opportunity to
explore the philosophical problems of knowledge.

TQ 1: Does Jack know that it was Harry who stole Ceebie and has he proved it?

Nested Questions:
- What is knowledge?
- When can we say we know something?
- How do we know that we know?
- Is 'thinking you know something' the same as 'knowing something'?
- How do we know something if we were not there to see it?
- How can we know something if no one was there to see it?

The story continues ...

*Jack and his dad go to the school, to the head teacher's office where Ceebie is being kept. The head says that Ceebie has been caught stealing from the school and so must be held responsible. The head tells Jack and his dad that Ceebie must be dismantled. Jack starts to cry.*

*Then Jack has an idea. He suddenly looks up at the head and says, 'But what about fingerprints? If somebody else has programmed him then won't he have their fingerprints on him?'*

*They check for fingerprints and Ceebie has the fingerprints of three people: Jack, Tony and Harry. 'You see,' says Jack, 'It must have been Harry.'*

Here is another optional stop-point for discussion.

TQ 2: Is Jack right? Have they proved that it was Harry?

Nested Questions:
- What is proof?
- How do you prove something?
- Can you prove something 100 per cent for certain?

The story continues ...

*The head teacher explains regretfully: 'I am sorry Jack, but this only shows it could have been any of you. Also, has Harry been to your house for tea and touched Ceebie at all?'*

*Jack thinks about it for a minute and considers lying to get Harry into trouble – he is so sure that it's him. But then he thinks that lying would not help with anything. 'Yes, he did come round to mine and he touched Ceebie to program him to do a dance,' Jack admits while looking down at his feet.*

*'Then, I'm afraid it doesn't prove that Harry did it. Ceebie will still need to be dismantled,' says the head.*

*Then Jack's dad says: 'I may have an idea. If we were to access Ceebie's programming history on his hard drive might we find out some more information?'*

*The head thinks for a moment and finally says, 'Yes, maybe we could,' then asks for the school computer expert to come to his office.*

*After about half an hour of tapping away at the keyboard the computer expert says: 'Here we are: the last command issued to Ceebie says: "You will go to the school hall and take the charity donation box; then you will return to number 10 Barrel Street and hand over the money to ... Harry Miller."'*

'So,' *says the head teacher,* 'it seems we will need to pay a visit to Harry's house and speak to his parents.' *The head then turns to Jack and says:* 'You and Ceebie can go home and Ceebie will not have to be dismantled.'

'HOORAY!' *shouts Jack. Jack, his dad and Ceebie all go home together. Jack has not been this happy for a long time.*

To continue with the discussions around knowledge that emerged from the whodunit part of the story you should finish by asking the following Task Question.

> TQ 3: Did the evidence on Ceebie's hard drive prove that Harry is the culprit?

> Nested Question: If Harry is the culprit, does this mean that Jack did know when he said he knew? (This could also make a good Task Question though it is slightly more advanced.)

This is the place to introduce the second philosophical topic for this session. Make sure you can leave at least 15 minutes discussion on this. Alternatively, you could ask this question in a follow-up session.

> TQ 4: If it was Harry who re-programmed Ceebie, then who would be responsible for the crime of stealing the charity box?

You may choose to remind them of the salient details: that Ceebie is the one that *actually did* the crime but that he was re-programmed to do it by someone else. I find that this discussion can take all sorts of unexpected twists and turns; for instance, some children will see the father as responsible because he made Ceebie mobile by giving him arms and legs. This seems to be a confusion, which is common with children, between something's being a *causal factor* and it being *morally responsible*. Jack's dad was a causal factor in that there would have been no crime if he had not made Ceebie mobile but it would seem to be an odd leap to therefore think that this makes him morally culpable as his intentions in no way included the performing of a crime. Some may argue that his crime was one of negligence rather than criminal intention, however. I advise not to try to teach them this distinction as it is complex and requires a degree of moral understanding that is often absent with primary age children. But if they make this distinction themselves, which some of them may, it would then be appropriate to let it in to the conversation. If this happens it certainly helps to be aware of this yourself.

---

**Extension Activity:**

Read or tell the children the following scenario.

*Imagine that you are in trouble. You stole something because your friend told you to. When you are told off you tell the teacher it was someone else who told you to do it.*

> TQ 5: Who do you think would be responsible?

Nested Question:
- Is this situation like the situation with Ceebie?

---

To end the session read the following.

*A week or two later, Jack is in the car with his dad and he asks him: 'Dad, if Ceebie only does what he is programmed to do, does that mean that he is only my friend because he is programmed to be my friend?'*

*Jack's dad looks puzzled. He has no idea how to answer Jack's question.*

Jack's question can quite easily be turned into a Task Question or Set Question.

> Set Question: If Ceebie only does what he is programmed to do, does that mean that he is only Jack's friend because he is programmed to be his friend?

This could be used for a further discussion in the session or as part of another session. Alternatively it could be set as a question for children to take home with them (see below and Set Questions online).

### Hints and tips: Set Questions – philosophy never ends!

Philosophy is a continuous activity. This is true in a number of senses. It is continuous in that it does not have clear and definite answers in the way other subjects often do (see *Why Teach Philosophy*, on page 11); and it is continuous in that the big questions of philosophy are passed on from generation to generation, down through the years. Once the philosophical project has been grasped by a student it can enter all aspects of their life and the process of reflection is always active from then on. A philosopher turns their philosophical gaze to most of what falls within their consideration. This should be encouraged at the earliest stages of philosophical development, and one way this can be done is to provide the children with a Set Question to go away with to help them continue the philosophising. I often say to them: 'Take the question home with you and discuss it with parents, friends and family.' The Set Question should always be simple to say and to remember but with enough complexity and open-endedness for it to be philosophically fruitful. Set Questions can be found in the Nested and Emergent Questions from the session you have just run.

# Online

Main philosophy:
Plato and Knowledge
Spinoza and Determinism

Related philosophy:
Hobbes and Materialism
Locke and Free Will
Moral Philosophy
Socrates, Plato and Weakness of the Will
Sartre, de Beauvoir and Human Nature

### Related sessions

The Ring of Gyges (page 74)
The Happy Prisoner (page 93)
The Frog and the Scorpion (page 105)
The Little Old Shop of Curiosities (page 111)
Billy Bash (page 128)

# The Ceebie Stories: The Android

## Themes

Being human
Analogy
Personal identity

## The philosophy

Here the question of identity is reversed so that the children are brought to the question of what it is that makes us human. The word 'android' comes from the Greek *andro* (meaning 'man') and *oid* (meaning 'form'). For Aristotle it is 'rationality' that marks us from the animals; for existentialists it is 'choice'; and for others it is our 'moral capacity' that makes us human. There is also a distinction between 'human' and 'person'; as the children may point out, Ceebie may not be human but maybe he should be treated *like* a human. Here the children have identified something of Ceebie's 'personhood' as distinct from his humanity. If intelligence or rationality were the criteria for a human, then that would exclude non-rational humans such as babies and the mentally ill. Some even argue that the higher intelligence species such as higher primates and dolphins should be considered as 'persons' though they are clearly not 'human'. Others argue that it is precisely because of animals' lack of rationality that means that we should include them in our moral considerations; perhaps it is the 'capacity for suffering' that is the criterion for personhood when thought about in this way.

## Stimulus

*At the beginning of this story, Ceebie was just a television screen on top of a long pole with speakers to talk and sensors to hear. When he spoke it was with a strange metallic, grating sound. When Jack's dad realised that Jack wanted to take Ceebie out with him, he built Ceebie a robot-body with arms, legs and grabbing hands. Later, Jack was upset that many of the other children at school would make fun of Ceebie because he 'talked funny' and because he kept knocking things over as he moved clumsily about. First of all Jack's dad perfected Ceebie's voice so that it sounded like a normal boy's voice. If you weren't in the same room as Ceebie you would have thought there was real boy talking to Jack. It was quite amazing how real he sounded.*

*About a year later Jack's dad upgraded Ceebie once more. He constructed a new, more complex frame for him that he covered with fake plastic skin. When he had finished, Jack was astounded to see that Ceebie looked exactly like a real boy; his skin and hair looked real.*

*It was now almost impossible to tell that Ceebie was not a real boy, but there was one important way that the other children could still tell Ceebie wasn't human: he had no emotions. He never cried or got angry or scared or showed any signs of happiness. Jack's dad saw this as the final and ultimate challenge. He set to work.*

*He created an emotion-chip: a tiny little piece of computer technology that was to be put inside Ceebie's chest. This chip would enable Ceebie to display emotional responses, so, if he was left out of games for instance he would appear to feel left out and would appear to feel sad and if he appeared very sad he would cry.*

*It was now impossible to tell Ceebie apart from a real boy and because of this Jack decided to give him a name. He thought that he would name him to fit his initials: 'C' and 'B', so he named Ceebie 'Charles Brown' to make him sound more human and to help him 'fit in' with everyone a bit more easily.*

*Even though he looked human Jack's friends still called him 'the robot' and when they did it seemed to really upset Ceebie. One day he said to Jack, 'Everyone still calls me "the robot" and I don't like it. I want everyone to think of me as a human being, not a robot.'*

This story should be accompanied with the following diagrammatic illustrations to help the children see the various stages of Ceebie's development. 🖱

I usually explain that there is a word for a robot that looks and acts just like a human being: an *android* (many will know the word 'droid' from *Star Wars*.) The Task Question following this story is as follows.

TQ 1: Now that Ceebie looks and acts exactly like a human being and wants to be thought of as a human being, is Ceebie a human being?

Stage 1: Stationary computer; Stage 2: Robot body; Stage 3: Voice; Stage 4: New body with hair and skin etc.; Stage 5: Emotion chip; Stage 6: Name and thought of as human by others

Nested Questions:
- If so, then at what stage did Ceebie become human? (See *Sorites paradox*, page 87.)
- What do you need to be human?
- Can a computer think?
- Can a computer have feelings?
- Is Ceebie a boy or a girl or neither?

Almost invariably discussions on this story begin with the children unanimously agreeing that Ceebie is not human, though, as the discussion unfolds and develops, some of the children often begin to take a different view. Some think that, though a chip or computer cannot be a brain, it can serve a similar function as a brain. Some, therefore, take a view that understands Ceebie as being 'like a human' even if he is not a human.

> ### Teaching Strategy: Test the implications (page 40)
>
> With a class of children aged 5–6 we were discussing whether the brain and the mind are the same thing or different. One child said that

the mind is inside the brain. I then asked, making sure not to lead him to an answer, 'If the mind is inside the brain would the mind be the same as the brain or different?' He thought about this for a bit and then said, 'Different.' I immediately asked, 'Why?' and he replied quickly, 'Because the mind pours ideas into the brain.' I find that closed questions are useful, in a situation like this, to help children face the implications of their own ideas with greater clarity and precision. Here's an example.

A (Child): Ceebie is not alive because he doesn't have a heart.
B (Facilitator): Do you think you need a heart to be alive? (Closed question.)
A: Yes.
B: Why? (Opens up the question again.)
A: Because . . .

If you were to ask this in an 'open' way – that is, with open questions – the child could answer in a way that does not show a consideration for the formal argument. The technique of testing the implications of their ideas pinpoints them to a consideration for the argument in question. It is important to phrase the question so that it accurately reflects the child's first premise, so try not to paraphrase the terms and concepts that they use.

# Online

Main philosophy:
Sartre, de Beauvoir and Human Nature

Related philosophy:
Aristotle and Teleology
Descartes and Dualism
Hobbes and Materialism
Leibniz, Searle and Artificial Intelligence
Locke and Free Will

 **Related Sessions**

# The Ceebie Stories: The Lie

*For the 2010 Year 3 class at St. William of York Primary School, Lewisham.*

Star rating: ***

## Themes

Dilemmas
Decision-making
Values
Friendship
Lying

## The philosophy

This story provides the children with a classic dilemma where rules and obligations come into conflict with the instinct to protect one's friends. There are two philosophical areas that emerge from this story: that of *moral dilemmas*; and that of *moral luck*. Moral luck is related to whether the unforeseen outcomes or subsequent situations can alter the moral worth of an action. So, if you tell a lie but then circumstances transpire such that your lie turns out to be true, does that mean you did not tell a lie? Does it mean that your morally bad act (if it is bad) has turned into a morally good one? Can the moral worth of an action depend on luck?

## Stimulus

*Jack, Tony and Ceebie are now best friends. They have created a gang of three called 'The Droids'. They decide to make a den for their gang and to write a contract for the members of their gang. In their contract it says, 'We promise never to lie no matter what the consequences.' Jack wanted this in the contract after he was tempted to lie when he was asked by the head teacher if Harry had been to his house. Ceebie asks Jack to program the rules of the contract into him.*

*One day when they are playing in the den and making some improvements Ceebie says he is running low on power and needs to go home to re-charge. Tony says he has to go home to have his tea, so he offers to walk Ceebie back leaving Jack to finish off a few things in the den.*

*On their way home Tony and Ceebie see Billy Bash, the school bully, coming towards them. He has seen them, so there is no point running away. Billy is friends with Harry and has wanted to get Jack for some time in revenge for what happened to Harry after the incident with the charity box. When he sees Tony and Ceebie coming from the direction of the woods he thinks he might be able to find Jack.*

*'Is Jack back there in the woods?' he asks them, pointing to where they had just come from.*

*Tony and Ceebie both think that Jack is still in the den. If they answer 'yes' they think Jack will get beaten up by Billy, but if they answer 'no' then they will have told a lie and broken their promise to each other: never to lie no matter what the consequences.*

Stop the story here to present the dilemma Task Question. If you have read or told the story well, the children will probably have anticipated the dilemma as you were describing the situation. If so you may well hear a few gasps as it dawns on them.

TQ 1: What do you think Tony and Ceebie should decide to say to Billy Bash?

Nested Questions:
- When, if ever, is it okay to lie or break a promise?
- Are there any rules that should never be broken, no matter what?
- Is Ceebie wrong to tell the truth?

On a few occasions in sessions I have run, some children have suggested that they remain silent. This presents another wonderful Task Question.

TQ 2a: If Tony and Ceebie remain silent, then would they have lied or not?

## Extension Activity for older children: Thought experiment

Here is a more advanced thought experiment for older children to try if the issue of Ceebie having been programmed arises. This thought experiment tests our intuitions about lying and helps us to answer TQ 2 more carefully.

> TQ 2b: Ceebie has been programmed 'never to lie no matter what the consequences'. Would his programming allow Ceebie to remain silent?

Nested Question: What does this tell us about remaining silent and lying?

The story continues ...

*Tony thinks about it and decides to answer 'no', thinking it's better to tell a lie and break a promise than to let Billy beat Jack up. Ceebie, on the other hand, decides to answer 'yes' because he thinks it is wrong to lie and break a promise, as this rule has been programmed into him.*

*When Billy hears two different answers – 'No, he's not in the den' from Tony, and 'Yes, he is in the den' from Ceebie – he thinks that Jack must be there, so he runs off to find him with his fists clenched. Tony and Ceebie run home to get Jack's dad.*

*When Tony and Ceebie reach Jack's home they are shocked to find ... Jack sitting on the wall to his house swinging his legs and smiling smugly at them.*

*Tony says, 'How did you get here before us? Did you see Billy Bash?' Jack just smiles at them.*

*'Why are you not beaten up?' asks Ceebie.*

*'I don't know what you mean,' says Jack with a puzzled look on his face.*

*They explain everything that happened and Jack confesses that he had told them he was going to stay behind but really he had planned to run home by a different route so he could play a trick on them and get home before them. They realise that Jack must have left already by the time Billy arrived in the den. Jack suddenly turns to Ceebie and says: 'That means that you lied and Tony told the truth.' He thinks about it and then says, 'That's weird.'*

Before continuing with the session it is important to clarify the situation for the class with the following diagram, explaining it verbally as you draw it.

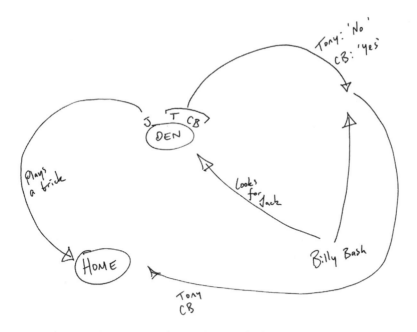

### Teaching Strategy: Web of understanding (page 43)

This story is complicated and particularly the second part where Tony and Ceebie are unaware that Jack has left the den. A diagram is essential at this stage to aid children's understanding, but if there are those who still struggle to understand the situation in the story then use the 'web of understanding' strategy. Ask who in the classroom thinks they understand what's going on. Choose somebody with their hand up to explain to the others. Then ask if there is anyone else who now understands and would like to explain, in their own words, what they think is going on. Try to choose someone who did not understand before. Intervene only when necessary – for instance, if an important misunderstanding is being communicated – and continue in this way until you have optimised the understanding among the whole class.

Here is a moral luck Task Question.

TQ 3: Is Jack right? Does this mean that Ceebie lied and Tony told the truth?

Nested Questions:
• What is a lie?
• Can you do a good thing (or a bad thing) by accident?

Some children may point out that Jack lied when he said he was going to stay in the den when he intended to go home by another route to surprise his friends. A good Task Question around this is given below.

> TQ 4: Did Jack lie when he said he was staying in the den but actually went home?

Nested Questions:
- Is there a difference between a trick or a joke and a lie? If so, what is the difference?
- Did Jack break the contract when he played the trick on them?
- Does a lie have to be intended as a lie?
- If you say something you believe is true and then it turns out to be wrong, does that mean that you have lied?

I have noticed that, certainly in the area of London where I work, many children will use the expression 'You lied' when they actually mean '*You made a mistake*'. Getting things wrong and telling lies are conceptually and significantly different, and a discussion around this can be very beneficial for the children to explore what is really involved in lying and how it is different from false belief.

## Extension Activity for older children ages 9–11

Imagine, sometime in the future, scientists invent a way to program us to behave in a certain way. They can now perform an operation to make us follow these rules.

1 You should not hurt people.
2 You should not steal.
3 You should not lie.

> TQ 5: Should you have the operation?

Nested Question:
- If not these, then are there other rules you should never break?

# Online

Main philosophy:
Kant and Moral Luck

Related philosophy:
Locke and Free Will
Moral Philosophy
Plato and Justice
Sartre, de Beauvoir and Human Nature
Socrates, Plato and Weakness of the Will
Spinoza and Determinism

 **Related sessions**

The Ring of Gyges (page 74)
The Frog and the Scorpion (page 105)
Billy Bash (page 128)

# The Ceebie Stories: The Rebuild

## Themes

Change
Personal identity
Materials

## The philosophy

This is a classic question of identity through time in the vein of *The Ship of Theseus* (page 86). It addresses the issue of *materialism* (see Hobbes and Materialism on the companion website), the view that things are reducible to their material constituents, that there is nothing more than material things in the universe. According to materialists, the mind is nothing more than the workings of the brain; and the self, would likewise, be nothing more than the working brain and body. This has implications for beliefs about the soul and its transmigration – for instance, in the idea of reincarnation. If we are nothing more than our material constituents, then when the body dies so does the self; it would therefore make no sense to conceive of a self that is independent of a body that could leave the body at the time of death and travel somewhere else. On the other hand, materialism fails to account for non-material things such as sensations and experiences, love or abstract entities such as numbers. So, could a mind be something like this and therefore irreducible to constituent material parts? This session develops some of the ideas that emerge from *The Ship of Theseus* session, such as we are the same person because of our memories (see pages 86–92).

# Stimulus

One day, Jack's dad said to Jack: 'I would like to copy Ceebie's memories onto a separate hard drive and then update them every few days.'

'Why?' Asked Jack.

'Because then if something were to happen to Ceebie we would have his memories stored on the hard drive and all we would need to do is put them into a new body. Ceebie will always be safe then.'

'Okay,' said Jack, a little puzzled. A few weeks later he would understand exactly what his dad had meant.

Ever since he had been caught re-programming Ceebie to commit the crime at the school, Harry had been plotting his revenge on Ceebie and Jack. He was always looking for an opportunity to take his revenge. One day, by chance, that opportunity arose.

Jack and Ceebie were out walking along the coastal cliff close to the town they lived in. Harry was up ahead of them playing on his own. He saw them before they saw him, so he hid behind some trees and waited for them to pass him by. When they had just passed him, Harry shot out quickly and silently and he pushed Ceebie off the edge of the cliff before Jack knew what was happening. Ceebie fell to the rocks below and smashed up into tiny pieces. Before any of the pieces could be collected the sea came in and washed them away.

Jack was devastated and he cried and cried. That night his dad came into his room and said, 'Jack. Don't be sad. Do you remember when I asked you if we could store Ceebie's memories onto a hard drive?'

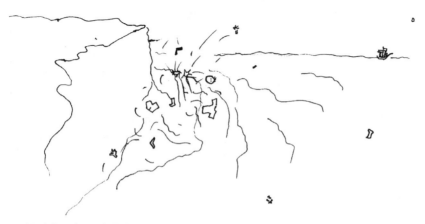

Ceebie fell to the rocks below and smashed up into tiny pieces

*'Yes. You said that Ceebie would always be safe if we did that,' recalled Jack.*

*'Exactly,' said his dad. 'I shall have Ceebie back for you in just a few weeks. I shall go to the factory tomorrow and start building a brand new body for Ceebie that will be exactly the same as the old one. I shall then install all the stored memories from the hard drive and Ceebie will be back as good as new.'*

*Jack stopped crying and again looked hopeful once more. He then hugged his dad. 'Thank you, dad, thank you!' he said.*

*Jack waited very patiently for a few weeks. It did take his dad longer than anticipated, but he worked on Ceebie's repairs harder than on anything else.*

*Eventually, Jack's dad came home from work and he entered the house with the new Ceebie following behind him. Jack was shocked and delighted to see Ceebie once more but he could not decide whether this was the same Ceebie or a different one. He remembered everything they had done together but Jack wasn't sure.*

> TQ 1: Is the new Ceebie the same as the old Ceebie?

It is very likely that there will be divided opinion about the material stuff that Ceebie is made from and how this affects his identity. Some may think that he can't be the same Ceebie if he is made from different parts ('He's not the same *actual* one' as one 9 year-old girl said) whereas others will think that the parts don't really matter if the memories are the same.

 **Teaching Strategy: Either/or the if – 'Let's think about it both ways' (page 42)**

The conditional form allows the facilitator and children to explore situations that are not true by virtue of the logical structure of the question: 'If … then …?' The disjunctive, 'Either … or …' allows you to explore alternative conditional situations or ideas. The two work well together to extend the reach of hypothetical thinking, which is one of the key areas of thinking that doing philosophy seeks to develop. In order to compare and contrast two different situations or ideas, you can hypothesise them both to see what the children think about them.

Situation A: Imagine that Ceebie's parts were collected and then he was built again from the same parts once they were repaired. Would this mean that the new Ceebie was the same as the old one?

Situation B: Imagine that Ceebie's parts were lost (as in the story) and so he was rebuilt with different parts but following the same plans and with the same memories as before. Would this mean that the new Ceebie was the same as the old one?

### Extension Activity

TQ 2: Do you think that the mind is the same thing as the brain or different?

# Online

Related philosophy:
Berkeley and Idealism
Descartes and Dualism
Heraclitus and Change
Hobbes and Materialism
Leibniz and Identity
Leibniz, Searle and Artificial Intelligence

### Related sessions

Can You Step in the Same River Twice? (page 61)
The Ship of Theseus (page 86)
Yous on Another Planet (page 139)
Where Are You? (page 182)
Get Stuffed: Fun with Metaphysics (page 186)

# The Ceebie Stories: Finally Human?

This is a short reprise of the themes that were present in the story *The Android*. It adds one more important dimension – self-conception – and adds it to the mix.

## The Stimulus

*When Jack tells his dad what Ceebie has said to him his dad says, 'I think I can solve that problem.' He takes Ceebie back to the factory and re-programmes him so that Ceebie no longer believes he is a robot; Ceebie now believes that he is human. His dad says to Jack, 'It is very important that nobody calls him "Ceebie" or refers to him as "a robot"; everyone should now call him by his human name: "Charles Brown" or, better still, "Charlie". Okay?'*

*'Okay,' says Jack, 'I promise.'*

*'From now on Charlie will be known as your brother,' instructs his father.*

*'Hooray,' shouts Jack, 'I finally have a real brother.' He had always wanted a brother or a sister.*

> TQ 1: Now that Ceebie looks human, believes he is human and everyone treats him as a human, is he finally human?

An important element for children is the role of the brain when considering what makes us human. Some children will think it essential that to be human there must be a brain. However, others will hold that as long as there is something to perform the same function as the brain, such as a microchip containing memories etc., then it does not matter if there is a brain or not. Some will think that a microchip may allow a computer to think but it may not be human. But the big question in this session is whether Ceebie/Charlie's own self-conception will decide this matter. With older children (ages 10 and upwards) you could turn this on them and ask them what they would think if they found out that they were an android. (See also *Yous on Another Planet*, page 139.)

# Online

Related philosophy:
Aristotle and Friendship
Berkeley and Idealism
Descartes and Dualism
Heraclitus and Change
Hobbes and Materialism
Leibniz and Identity
Leibniz, Searle and Artificial Intelligence

 **Related session**

The Meaning of Ant Life (page 57)
The Prince and the Pig (page 80)
The Frog and the Scorpion (page 105)
The Little Old Shop of Curiosities (page 111)
Yous on Another Planet (page 139)
The Ceebie Stories: The Android (page 162)

# To the Edge of Forever

*For the 2009 Year 5 classes at Eliot Bank Primary School, Lewisham.*

Suitable for age 7 and upwards.
Star rating: **

The story can be used with most classes age 7 and upwards, but I would recommend only using *Lucretius's Spear* argument with children from age 9 and upwards.

## Themes

Arguments
Infinity

## The philosophy

One of the most common philosophical ideas to cross children's minds often quite spontaneously is that of infinity. How can numbers go on forever? What's bigger than infinity? Does space go on forever? These are just some of the question formulations children make regarding infinity. So, it is good to exploit this natural philosophical concern that children have and to get them to think about it more deeply.

## Stimulus

*Methuselah is a scientist and philosopher who is very interested in the idea of 'forever'. And this year he is mostly thinking about whether the universe goes on forever or whether it has an edge. So, he decides to build a robot that can repair itself and he puts it in a space ship that is specially designed so that it does not need any new fuel – it has an ever-lasting battery! He then prepares the robot and the ship for the journey and on a Saturday afternoon in the year 2010 he launches the spaceship. He is sad that he will never be able to find out what the robot discovers but he sits down and thinks to himself about what he thinks the robot will discover.*

TQ 1: What do you think the robot will discover? That space goes on forever or do you think it will have an edge?

I have included this second part to the question to help keep the answers conceptually focused.

Nested Questions:
- Is the universe infinite?
- Is there another alternative to the options given above? For instance, could it be in some way circular or rounded?

# Lucretius' argument

This argument is available on the companion website.

The Roman philosopher Lucretius thought that the universe is infinite, and here are the reasons *why* he thought so.

First of all, Lucretius asks us to imagine a person who is able to walk all the way to the edge of the universe and then, when they get there, throw a spear across the boundary. Lucretius argues the following.

## The argument

The universe is infinite because …

If the spear hits a barrier or an edge then there must be something beyond that edge.

And, if it doesn't hit a barrier then the Universe must keep going. So, either way, it must be infinite.

TQ 2: Do you agree with Lucretius's reasons for why he thinks the universe is infinite, or not?

### Philosophy: The *a priori* 'It's logical!'

Philosophy is concerned with logic, meaning and understanding; it is not so concerned with what happens to be the case; that is, the concern of the natural sciences. If a discussion becomes concerned with what the facts happen to be, then the discussion has left the realm of philosophy. Philosophers distinguish between two types of concern:

empirical (the facts) and *a priori* (logical/conceptual). It might seem that a question like 'Is the universe infinite?' is an empirical question that science may one day be able to answer and until then there's not much we can say. However, there is a conceptual aspect to this question: 'Does it make *sense* to think of an infinite universe?' 'What are the implications of the idea of an infinite universe?' 'Does it make sense to think that science will one day answer this question?' You do not need to go to the edge of the universe to consider these questions because they are conceptual in nature and not factual. Here is a good example of this distinction emerging from a discussion with some children aged 10 and 11. The Task Question being discussed was: Is the universe infinite?

Anton began by saying that it is impossible for the universe to go on forever because there would then be too much space for the planets so they wouldn't be able to stay still. Notice that this argument has an *a priori* structure – that is, it is an argument that tries to answer the question just by thinking about it.

Max said that one cannot know the answer because it would take a spaceship too long to get there and you would die. Max has understood the question in an empirical way and has concluded that it is therefore unanswerable. Although, it is a related conceptual point about the limits of our knowledge that an infinite universe, would by definition, be impossible to discover to be infinite.

I then asked Anton and Max if they thought you would need to go the edge of the universe to find out if it is infinite or not. Max said that you would have to.

Leela then said that she thinks you don't have to go to the edge of the universe to answer the question. 'It can be answered,' she said, 'just by thinking about it in the same way that you can answer what the sum 6 x 8 is.' This means that Leela thinks it is an *a priori* question – that is, a logical, conceptual question.

# Online

Main philosophy:
Zeno, Paradoxes and Infinity

Related philosophy:
Aristotle and the Logical Syllogism
Frege, Russell and Logic
Leibniz and Identity

Metaphysics: What There Is
St. Augustine and Time
The Pre-Socratics and Natural Philosophy

 **Related sessions**

# Where Are You?

*For the 2009 Year 4 class at All Saints Primary School, Lewisham.*

Suitable for age 8 and upwards.
Star rating: **

## Themes

Personal identity
Who am I?
Minds and brains

## The philosophy

Where is the locus of the self? The ancient Egyptians thought that it was in the heart and for this reason they discarded the brain during the embalming process thinking it unimportant for the after-life. Intuitively we tend to think that we are in our head, perhaps because we look out from our eyes, so it seems we are behind our eyes. In modern science it has become the standard view that the self is located in the brain. This thought experiment introduces this idea to the children for them to consider for themselves. It is interesting how some children see themselves as their body and others as their brain and many discussions will polarise in this way, although there is another option which has emerged more recently in discussions about this topic: that the self is a composite of many different aspects of our body and its workings; an interrelationship of everything from the brain to the heart, the nervous system and the emotions. According to this view it is impossible to have a disembodied brain that still functions as a self in the way that we understand this to mean. This view is less likely in the classroom but listen out for it, or a version of it, usually present within the group as a whole rather than as the view of one particular child. (That makes this idea rather like the notion of the self this view is about!) Some will see the self as a separate thing from the mind or the brain and some may introduce the concept of the soul, so this session can become very rich and diverse. *Remember:* approach these discussions with sensitivity and allow the children to explore these ideas freely without judgement.

# Stimulus

*Imagine, sometime in the far future, there are two friends, Jenny and Alma, and they are very different kinds of people: Jenny is popular and pretty, and Alma is studious and intelligent but each is jealous of the other. So much so that they each want to be the other person. Eventually they decide to both go along to a company called 'Brain Swaps Limited' where they undergo an operation in which their brains are taken out of their bodies and then replaced in the other girl's body: Jenny's body now has Alma's brain and Alma's body has Jenny's brain.*

Draw a diagram such as this to help the children understand:

Where is Jenny and where is Alma?

TQ 1: Where is Jenny and where is Alma?

Nested Questions:
- Have they now achieved what they wanted: to become the other girl?
- Would Jenny still be Jenny and would Alma still be Alma?

- Would they be in each other's body? Or would Jenny simply have Alma's thoughts and vice versa?
- Are we our brain or are we our body?
- What is the self?
- Is it different or the same as the brain or body?

## Extension Activities: Who am I?

Draw on the board a large picture of a person with plenty of room to write words inside. Ask the children to think of all the things that make them who they are. Provide a couple of examples to demonstrate the range of characteristics you expect: 'guitarist' and 'curious', or 'British' and 'tall'. If you have time or would like to extend this over a couple of sessions, then they could draw their own portraits and fill them in themselves. Try to encourage a wide variety of answers.

The next stage is to *categorise* the list so that it becomes reduced to general features such as 'preferences/aversions' (explain these terms), 'physical characteristics', 'personality traits' etc. These portraits make good classroom displays and can be referred to for further discussion purposes. The aim is for the children to realize that there is more to who they are than what we look like and what we like to eat.

> TQ 2: Can you find something on this list that, if you took it away, you would not be *you* anymore? (See *sine qua non* below and on page 45.)

## Teaching Strategy: Sine qua non (page 45)

This strategy is used to attempt to identify an essential feature of something. For instance, a swimming pool may or may not have a diving board, so this is not an essential feature of a swimming pool; neither is the chlorine in the water. However, arguably, water may be an essential feature. But water on its own does not make a swimming pool (see *What's needed and what's enough?*, page 33). Plato and Aristotle were both philosophers who thought that things had an essence to which the idea of those things could be reduced. They were *essentialists*, though of very different kinds.

In order to get the children to explore the concept of personhood ask the following question.

TQ 3: Would we become a different person if we were to swap with someone else the following things?

- Our lunch boxes.
- Our clothes.
- Our gender.
- Our skin colour.
- Our limbs.
- Our brains.

# Online

Main philosophy:
Descartes and Dualism
Socrates, Aristotle and the Soul

Related philosophy:
Berkeley and Idealism
Heraclitus and Change
Hobbes and Materialism
Leibniz and Identity
Leibniz, Searle and Artificial Intelligence

 **Related sessions**

The Ship of Theseus (page 86)
Yous on Another Planet (page 139)
The Ceebie Stories: The Android (page 162)
The Ceebie Stories: The Rebuild (page 172)
The Ceebie Stories: Finally Human? (page 176)

# Get Stuffed: Fun with Metaphysics

*For the 2007–2008 Year 6 class at Holy Trinity Primary School, Lewisham.*

> Suitable for age 8 and upwards.
> Star rating: ***

## Themes

Materials
Science

## The philosophy

I have used the word 'stuff' in place of the subject of 'substance' in metaphysics, and in this session we are concerned with the nature of substance. What kind of thing would it be? Would it be many tiny things or one big thing? If something is made of plastic, then the plastic has to be made of something, but then that something has to be made of something else such as atoms, but then the atoms have to be made of something else smaller again. The philosophical question is: Would this keep on going forever or would it have to stop at some point; and what kind of stuff would it be?

The ancient Greek philosopher Democritus (circa 460–370 BCE) thought that it was absurd to think that the discussion between Andy and Benny below (page 187) would continue forever. It would be impossible for each kind of stuff to be made of something else and on for infinity. So he hypothesised that there must be an entity that was basic and from which everything was made but which was not made of anything else. He named this entity 'atom', or 'indivisible' (from the Greek '*a*' meaning 'not' and '*tom*' coming from the Greek 'to cut'). A useful analogy to help illustrate this is to think of *Lego*. It has basic parts that stick together and from which lots of different things can be made even though the basic parts cannot be broken down any further.

# Stimulus

This dialogue could be read out or performed by two pupils.

*Andy:* I want to know what things are made of.
*Benny:* That's easy – everything is made of plastic or metal or wood ... I know: 'materials'.
*Andy:* But what are the materials made of?
*Benny:* Something smaller like atoms.
*Andy:* But what are the atoms made of?
*Benny:* Something smaller than atoms. I don't know. They are made of 'stuff'!
*Andy:* Yeah, but what kind of stuff?
*Benny:* I dunno! Just 'stuff'. Isn't that good enough?
*Andy:* Okay. Let's imagine that you're right: everything is made of stuff. What's the stuff made of?
*Benny:* More stuff!
*Andy:* But is it the same stuff or different stuff?
*Benny:* I don't know! But it's got to stop somewhere – there has to be something that is so small you can't get anything smaller.

> TQ 1: Will this discussion go on forever? Who do you agree with?

# The incredible shrinking machine

*Imagine you are an inventor who has invented an incredible shrinking machine. This machine is able to continue to shrink so that you can journey into the inner-world and see things as they are as you get smaller and smaller and smaller ...*

> TQ 2: Will you keep shrinking forever?

Nested Questions:
- Do you think you will ever find the smallest thing there is?
- Is there a smallest thing?
- Will you eventually shrink to nothing?
- Is there something so small there can't be anything smaller?
- Can something become nothing?

### Teaching Strategy: If the fact/idea (page 35)

You are very likely to encounter lots of objections to this thought experiment to do with the practical possibilities of shrinking. Use the *if the idea* strategy to meet these objections. Here's an example.

Objection: You couldn't keep shrinking because the air pressure would kill you.

Facilitator: (*if the idea*) Let's imagine that the air pressure won't kill you – *if* you could keep shrinking, do you think you would shrink forever or would you eventually vanish altogether?

### Extension Activity for older children: Democritus and the atom

This activity is for older children, aged 10 and upwards, or gifted and talented children. First explain the following.

*Democritus said that an atom is the smallest thing that can exist. Scientists discovered what they thought was the smallest thing that could exist and they named it an 'atom', after Democritus. In the early 20th century scientists successfully split the atom revealing that it was in fact made of smaller things.*

> TQ 3: Had the scientists proved Democritus wrong when they split the atom?

It is tempting to say that they had disproved Democritus when they split the atom but, as some children have pointed out, if they split the atom then Democritus may simply say, 'That clearly wasn't an atom because it was split, and an atom is *whatever it is that cannot be split.*' Democritus' atom is a *theoretical entity* only and therefore indivisible by definition, whereas the atom that was split was a *scientific entity*, something that was discovered and then given the name 'atom'.

## Teaching Strategy: Sympathise and criticise (page 45)

Introduce the children to the earlier Greek philosopher Thales (circa 624–546 BCE) and his view that 'everything is made of water'. Begin by asking them why he might have thought this and set them the task of coming up with all the reasons they can why they think he might be right. In other words, get them to sympathise with his view. They can then go away and consider this in groups. For example, they may say, 'Water is in most things' or 'Water is essential for life' etc.

Once this has been explored ask them to consider what they think might be wrong with this view. In other words, ask them to criticise Thales' view. Children I have worked with have suggested the following: 'If you look at that table it is not made of water and if it was it would just flow away' or 'If plants are made of water then they wouldn't need water like they do because they are already made of water'.

## Extension Activity: Atoms

Here's something for the class to think about.

Eve's (age 10) argument:

'The eye cannot see an atom. If everything is made of atoms then when I look at my hand I should see nothing.'

Display this argument on the board and ask the children what they think of it. (Also available on the companion website.)

This conundrum was solved by another child in the class, Henry (age 10) when he said: 'The eye can't see *an atom* but it can see *atoms*.'

# Online

Main philosophy:
Metaphysics: What There Is

Related philosophy:
Berkeley and Idealism
Heraclitus and Change
Hobbes and Materialism

Kant and the 'Thing In Itself'
The Pre-Socratics and Natural Philosophy
Zeno, Paradoxes and Infinity

 **Related Sessions**

# Glossary

The glossary includes, in brackets, the abbreviations used in this book for the terms that are explained. Where you see ⌁ you will find more detail regarding that particular term on the companion website.

**Comprehension Time**: a short period of time at the beginning of an enquiry where the children are given time to express and explore their understanding of the narrative element of a story or stimulus. When questions are asked, as often as possible, the other children are given the task of answering the questions. This helps them to build their own understanding of stimuli using their own language and register. The teacher intervenes only when necessary to clarify misunderstandings.

**Concept**: an abstract idea that underpins and informs all forms of thinking from perception to language and reasoning. Consider a square: if you draw a square you only have an imperfect image of a square; if you try to find a square in the world it is almost impossible to find something that is a perfect square (e.g. the edges will not be exactly straight). However, when you think of a square or try to define a square, then you are dealing with the *concept* of a square, the image of which is only a representation.

**Critical thinking skills**: the skills required to be able to engage with a stimulus critically. The word 'critical' is not necessarily meant negatively, but so that the student's engagement with the material challenges what is being presented to them. This approach tests the robustness of any ideas, arguments or opinions and insists that the originator of the idea or ideas rethink their position when necessary according to the demands of reason.

**Dewey, John**: An American philosopher (1859–1952) very interested in educational reforms. He advocated active engagement of students with their learning in contrast to the 'empty vessel' model of teaching where students are seen as something into which information and knowledge is 'poured'. He saw education as the beginning of its citizen's involvement in the democratic process and his community of enquiry method was devised to provide students with a forum to exercise their democratic rights from the very beginning of their education.

**Dialectic**: a collaborative process of discussion comprised of reasonable ideas, responses, objections and replies had by two or more people with the aim of exploring an idea in order to find the truth together, or to reach clarity of some kind regarding the idea in question. ⌐

**Dialogue**: this is the process held between interlocutors that consist of statements, objections, replies and supporting comments. It is the conversational element of the philosophical process and allows dialectic to develop.

**Emergent Questions (EQ)**: the questions that have not been prepared but have either been asked by the children in the course of the enquiry or that have been identified and formulated by the facilitator from comments the children have made. ⌐

**Enquiry**: a collective endeavour to explore and investigate a particular idea together in a focussed way. ⌐

**Fallacious argument**: an argument that has the superficial appearance of being good because of its structure, but which contains errors of reasoning.

**First thoughts**: this is a period of a few minutes to let the children reflect spontaneously on the stimulus before introducing a Task Question. This is a good time for the children to answer each other's comprehension questions about the stimulus. ⌐

**Hypothetical thinking**: this makes use of conditional and counter-factual questions. A *conditional* question or sentence is of the form 'if ... then ...'. The 'if' part of the sentence provides the conditions under which the 'then' part of the sentence is said to be the case. A *counter-factual* is a conditional question (or sentence) that considers a situation that is not factually true (counter to the facts), such as: 'If everyone was a vegetarian then would that make eating meat wrong?'

**Nested Questions (NQ)**: the implicit questions that lie behind a *Task Question* or within a stimulus. You do not have to ask these questions, but they can be asked if they emerge from the discussion. ⌐

**Plato**: Ancient Greek philosopher (427–348 BCE) who was taught by Socrates and himself taught Aristotle. He wrote about education a number of times in his works but perhaps most notably in his dialogue the *Meno* in which the character of Socrates discusses the nature of virtue and learning by way of a demonstration with a slave boy. Plato wanted to show that knowledge does not come from outside of us to be 'put in' to us, but is something already within us that can be 'recollected' by the use of good questioning from a teacher. This has been highly influential in theories of teaching and pedagogy and is still influential today.

**Philosophical enquiry (PhiE)**: a method for exploring philosophical ideas together using questions and reasoning.

**Philosophy**: from the ancient Greek words for 'love' (*philo*) and 'wisdom' (*sophia*) literally meaning 'the love of wisdom or learning'. It is also a special subject studied at universities that explores ideas about three broad areas of inquiry: *metaphysics*, *epistemology* and *ethics* or, in other words and respectively, *what there is* (reality), *what we can know about what there is* (knowledge) and *what matters in what there is* (value). Philosophy is concerned with logical, conceptual thinking and reasoning and is often more about understanding problems than about answering questions though many questions are asked in philosophy. When answers are sought one is seeking for *possible* answers.

**Response Question (RQ)**: this is a suggested question to ask a child in response to an expected idea. The main idea of these is to give a general feel for how to question in a philosophy session, they are not meant to be literally 'remembered and asked' though you can use them if you want. ⌁

**Set Questions (SQ)**: these are the questions that you may set for the children to continue thinking about between sessions. They may also be encouraged to discuss these questions with their parents, teachers, friends and family or be set as a written homework for their philosophy journals. ⌁

**Socrates**: teacher of Plato and one of the most famous philosophers because of his memorable biography. After becoming decorated for his bravery in the Peloponnesian wars between Athens and Sparta, he eschewed wealth and status for a simple life engaging the people of Athens in challenging philosophical discussions. This eventually led to his being taken to court and put on trial by certain powerful citizens of Athens who disliked his disquieting habit of getting the young people of Athens to think for them selves. He was found guilty of corrupting the minds of the young and for preaching false gods; he was sentenced to death and he accepted his sentence with equanimity (though he contested the charges) and died surrounded by his friends (including Plato) after drinking a cup of poisonous hemlock.

**Socratic irony**: the practice by Socrates of assuming a position of ignorance in order to elicit thoughts and ideas from his interlocutors.

**Stimulus**: that which is presented to a group (usually in a story form) to stimulate thinking and discussion and to help set the philosophical arena and around which the Task Questions are set.

**Talk Time (TT)**: This is the time given for the children to talk to each other in pairs or groups either before or during an enquiry.

**Task Questions (TQ)**: the main question around which an enquiry is focussed and which is designed to set a philosophical arena for the PhiE.

**Thought experiments**: experiments undertaken with thought alone where the aim is to test ideas against our intuitions.

# Bibliography

Asimov, Isaac. (1976). *Bicentennial Man*. USA: Random House Inc.

Asimov, Isaac. (1950). *I, Robot*. USA: Gnome Press.

Fisher, Robert. (1997). *Games for Thinking*. UK: Nash Pollock Publishing.

Turing, Alan. (1950). *Computing Machinery and Intelligence*. UK: Alan Turing.

# Useful Websites

## UK training

The Philosophy Shop
For further training in enquiry, more enquiry resources and specialist philosophy teachers visit:
http://www.thephilosophyshop.co.uk

SAPERE: Society for the Advancing Philosophical Enquiry and Reflection in Education
An educational charity dedicated to promoting the use of philosophy for children/communities throughout the UK and teacher training; visit:
http://www.sapere.org.uk

For training in Scotland visit: http://www.strath.ac.uk/humanities/courses/education/courses/pgcertphilosophywithchildren/

## International training and websites supporting philosophy with children and in the community

EPIC: European Philosophical Inquiry Centre
The website of Dr Catherine McCall, who collaborated with Matthew Lipman and whose work was featured on the 1990 BBC documentary *Socrates for Six Year Olds*:
http://www.epic-original.com

IAPC: Institute for the Advancement of Philosophy for Children – USA
http://cehs.montclair.edu/academic/iapc/

ICPIC: International Council of Philosophical Inquiry with Children – USA
http://www.icpic.org

Federation of Australasian Philosophy in Schools Associations
http://www.fapsa.org.au

Menon
MENON is a project of 11 European partners, which aims to encourage teachers' professional growth by developing their dialogical sensitivity and skills through philosophical enquiry:
http://menon.eu.org

SOPHIA: The European Foundation for the Advancement of Doing Philosophy with Children.
For Teachers, philosophers and educators working in the field of philosophy with children:
http://www.sophia.eu.org